LEARN TO PLAY
like the GUITAR GREATS

LEARN TO PLAY
like the GUITAR GREATS
THE ESSENTIAL GUIDE TO CHORDS, EQUIPMENT, AND TECHNIQUES

Charlotte Greig

BARNES & NOBLE BOOKS

NEW YORK

This edition published by Barnes & Noble, Inc.,
by arrangement with Amber Books Ltd
2005 Barnes & Noble Books

ISBN 0-7607-6962-1

Editorial and design by
Amber Books Ltd
Bradley's Close
74–77 White Lion Street
London N1 9PF
www.amberbooks.co.uk

Project Editor: James Bennett
Design: Zoë Mellors
Picture Research: Terry Forshaw, Natasha Jones
Music and Rights Consultants: James Sleigh and
Andrew King at Artemis Music
Studio Photography: Mal Stone
Model: Tom Fleming

M 10 9 8 7 6 5 4 3 2 1

Printed in Singapore

Cover Picture Credits:
Front cover (from left): Jimi Hendrix (Robert Knight/Redferns); Eric
Clapton (Ebet Roberts/Redferns); Bo Diddley (Michael Ochs/
Redferns); Slash (Mick Hutson/Redferns); Jimmy Page (Ian
Dickson/Redferns); Gibson supplied courtesy of Gibson Guitar Corp.
Back cover: Ritchie Blackmore (Ebet Roberts/Redferns)

Contents

INTRODUCTION

Over the last fifty years one instrument has come to dominate popular

music: the guitar. Whether it's the electric guitar, as wielded by rock

legends from Jimmy Page to Kurt Cobain, and blues legends from

BB King to Stevie Ray Vaughan, or the acoustic guitar as

strummed by folk artists from Woody Guthrie to Nick Drake,

it's the instrument that defines the sound of our times.

RIGHT *The hollow-bodied acoustic guitar remains a popular and practical instrument for guitar students and professionals.*

Playing the guitar is about more than just learning chords and notes: it's about respect for tradition and learning from the masters. Accordingly, in this book we've set out to teach you not only the mechanics of playing the guitar, but also to introduce you to the wider culture of guitar playing.

Here, for the first time in one volume, you can learn about the histories of rock, blues, folk, jazz and country guitar playing, then find out about the lives and techniques of all the greatest pickers – all the way from roots pioneers like Robert Johnson and Maybelle Carter, right up to contemporary heroes like Slash and Jack White – and then follow step-by-step instructions which will help you to play their greatest riffs. And along the way you can find out everything you need to know about the instrument and its associated equipment, from when the first electric guitar was built to how many pedals Pink Floyd's Dave Gilmour could fit into one effects unit.

FAR LEFT *The classic Fender Stratocaster is an all-electric model associated with a wide range of pop and rock artists, from Hank Marvin to Jimi Hendrix.*

LEFT *Semi-acoustics like this Washburn combine the qualities of both electric and acoustic guitars, and are a popular choice for country and folk artists.*

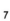

ROCK AND POP GUITARISTS

Just as rock music itself evolved out of other pre-existing musical forms – rhythm & blues and country music in particular – so rock guitar emerged from a variety of sources. The dominant influence may have been electric blues guitar playing, but there are also definite influences from country guitar playing and from mainstream pop.

BELOW: *Carlos Santana lays into a guitar riff. Santana began learning the guitar at age eight, entering professional music just after he finished high school.*

Above all, though, the rise of rock guitar is intimately connected with technology. Rock was the first music to grow up with the electric, rather than the acoustic, guitar as the standard instrument. The first electric guitars had been around since the 1920s, but it was only with T-Bone Walker's adoption of the electric guitar in a blues context, in the early 1940s, that the roots of rock guitar playing can really begin to be seen. Walker and his successors – bluesmen like B.B. King, John Lee Hooker and Muddy Waters – began to demonstrate the awesome power and volume the electric guitar could offer.

Meanwhile, in the field of country music, players like Merle Travis and Chet Atkins were developing a more melodic finger-picked electric style. Gradually, during the 1950s, the two styles began to come together. You can hear them both at work in the guitar playing of Scotty Moore with Elvis Presley. Moore was a country picker raised in the Merle Travis school, but he was recording in the same Sun Studios where a host of electric bluesmen had worked, and their influence most certainly rubbed off on him.

Another key player in the development of rock guitar was Bo Diddley. Bo Diddley came out of a rhythm & blues background, but his idiosyncratic additions of Cuban rhythm and full-on showmanship, plus a knack for the catchy nursery rhyme-simple song, proved a huge influence on rockers to come.

Then there was Chuck Berry. If there's a single inventor of rock guitar playing, it has to be Chuck Berry. He took blues and country and melded them together in a defiantly original, deceptively simple, style that was to provide the building blocks for everything that was to follow. All the early rock guitarists – from Buddy Holly to Cliff Gallup to James Burton – were disciples of the great Berry.

The flame of rock died down considerably in the USA during the late 1950s. For a while rock guitar seemed to appear only on instrumental recordings – Link Wray's sinister 'Rumble', Lonnie Mack's 'Memphis', a whole heap of Duane Eddy records – before surf music arrived in the early 1960s, and the likes of Jan And Dean and The Beach Boys once more raided Chuck Berry's riff larder.

SOUNDTRACK TO A GENERATION

For most of the next decade rock guitar – and rock music generally – would be dominated by musicians from across the Atlantic. Rock 'n' roll had a huge impact in the UK, and a generation of teenagers started learning Chuck Berry riffs – among them the likes of George Harrison, Keith Richards, Jimmy Page and Ritchie Blackmore. They all started out playing Chuck Berry covers in local bands, and by the early 1960s, they had started to get pretty good at it. Gradually, too, they started to write their own material.

Leaders in the field were, of course, The Beatles. Prior to The Beatles, rock 'n' roll and teen pop had always featured a pretty boy standing at the front, with the musicians kept well in the background. The Beatles ushered in the era of the band. Typical bands were four- or five-piece combos with vocalist, bassist and drummer plus either one or two guitarists. Steadily the role of the guitarist began to rival that of the singer in importance.

Despite their fame, The Beatles may not be thought of as a guitar band, but the guitar playing of John Lennon and particularly George Harrison was to become hugely influential. Harrison's knack for a catchy riff or an interesting fill inspired thousands of guitarists to follow in his wake.

The guitar became even more prominent in the work of The Beatles' great rivals, The Rolling Stones. Signature Stones' songs

ABOVE: *Chuck Berry performs his legendary 'duck walk' guitar step. He said he created the step in 1956, originally to hide the creases in a rayon suit.*

like 'Satisfaction' were driven by the guitar riffs, and Keith Richards was seen by many fans as the real heart of the band.

While the likes of Harrison and Richards tried to combine their love of R&B and blues with the demands of a pop career, other young British guitar players were getting ever deeper into the blues. The first of these to really make a name for himself was Eric Clapton, though others, like Peter Green, soon followed. The original guitar hero, Clapton was inspired by American bluesmen like Freddie King, and his virtuosity on his instrument made him the star of every band he was in. As the 1960s moved on, and the album market began to develop, Clapton and his followers were able to stretch out and solo for as long as they liked.

If Clapton's playing sometimes veered towards the self-indulgent, and was certainly angled more at his fellow musicians than the mass of pop fans, the next great guitarist to emerge showed that technical brilliance could be allied to rock 'n' roll showmanship. His name was Jimi Hendrix and his impact on rock guitar playing is unrivalled. Here was a man who understood that the electric guitar was not just an acoustic guitar with a pickup, but an instrument in its own right with its own extraordinary sonic potential.

Other guitar players were quick to exploit the new sonic territory that Hendrix opened up. Jimmy Page, a versatile former session musician, formed Led Zeppelin and combined delicate folk-derived playing with fiery full-on electric assaults. Jeff Beck, thought by many to be the most technically gifted of all the classic rock guitarists, gradually fused jazz influences into his playing. Others, like Ritchie Blackmore of Deep Purple and Tony Iommi of Black Sabbath, opted for a simplified style known as heavy metal, in which the riff was king.

ABOVE: *Jimmy Page joined forces with singer Robert Plant to create legendary riffs such as 'Whole Lotta Love' and student guitarists' all-time favourite, 'Stairway to Heaven'.*

A NEW BREED OF GUITAR HEROES

By the late 1960s American guitarists had responded convincingly to the British invasion. The Grateful Dead's Jerry Garcia developed a style of psychedelic rock playing that drew heavily on the folk and country tradition. The Allman Brothers' Duane Allman and Dickey Betts brought soul and jazz influences into a southern rock style. Texan Johnny Winter offered a blistering blues attack, while California's Carlos Santana fused Latin American influences into his melodic post-Hendrix style.

In the late 1970s rock music went through a period of re-evaluation. The rock gods of the previous decade had become increasingly self-indulgent and punk rock came along to take rock back to basics. The new breed of rock guitar heroes to emerge in the next decade were typically disciplined, focused players who understood the demands of the song. Such players included the supreme hard rock technician Eddie Van Halen, and the much more technically limited, but undeniably effective, The Edge from U2. Nile Rodgers also demonstrated that the guitar had a place at the heart of funk, while Prince showed that boundaries between funk, rock, pop and psychedelia were all imaginary if you had the nerve – and the talent – to cross them.

Perhaps the definitive late 1980s guitar hero was Slash from Guns n' Roses. His riff for 'Sweet Child O' Mine', along with his wholesale appropriation of the Keith Richards rock 'n' roll swagger, marked something of a last hurrah for the traditional guitar hero.

During the 1990s the music business became increasingly diffuse. It was no longer possible to talk of rock as being a single entity. Different strands – punk, metal, nu-metal, country-rock, post-rock, roots-rock – all flourished alongside each other, their followers barely aware of each other's existence. So, too, the styles of rock guitar became more varied. At one extreme a new kind of 'guitar player's guitar player' emerged – phenomenally gifted musicians like Steve Vai and Joe Satriani who have huge followings among guitar buffs, yet are almost unknown to the general public. At the other extreme were musicians like Kurt Cobain and The White Stripes' Jack White who proudly displayed their punk credentials and disdain for musical snobbery. Meanwhile guitarists like Sonic Youth's Thurston Moore tried their utmost to take sonic exploration to its outer limits.

With such a wide breadth of guitar styles to choose from today, one might feel that there is not a whole lot of new territory to explore. However, all aspiring guitarists have to begin by choosing a style or styles to imitate; then, if they

LEFT: *Keith Richards of the Rolling Stones studied the work of early blues guitarists in the early 1960s to develop his distinctive style and tunings.*

have the talent, they will go on to create their own style. If they do, they will find that even today, there is always room for that indefinable element that makes a 'guitar great': originality.

KEEPING IN THE BACKGROUND

Playing rock guitar isn't always about taking centre stage and pulling dramatic poses. Rock and pop music are ultimately song-based and some of the form's consummate craftspeople are those guitarists who would hate for you to be distracted by their playing, and who put all their talent at the service of expressing the song. Perhaps the ultimate example of this type of musician is the guitarist from the all-time definitive pop/rock group, The Beatles. As a guitarist George Harrison was the ultimate team player. Lennon and McCartney may have hogged the limelight but without George's support they wouldn't have been nearly so successful. Time and time again, Harrison crafted intros, fills and lead lines that were as hook-laden as the songs themselves. He opened John Lennon's rocker 'A Hard Day's Night' with a single ringing G7sus4 chord, in the process creating one of the most celebrated introductions in rock. Throughout 1964 and 1965, Harrison uncorked one Rickenbacker riff after another, from the descending fills of 'Help' to the ear-grabbing opening in 'Ticket to Ride'. It's hard to imagine those songs without the sections George created. Divorce any one of them from the track, and the song just doesn't sound right.

When rock took a more aggressive turn in 1966, Harrison once again switched instruments, acquiring a Gibson SG and announcing his presence with authority on McCartney's 'Paperback Writer', the toughest-sounding A-side in The Beatles' collection. On *Revolver*, Harrison's experimental nature led to yet another new wrinkle: backwards guitar.

Even as the artistic and personal distance between Lennon and McCartney increased in later years, Harrison's guitar work continued to create the impression of a unified group. From *Sgt. Pepper* forward, the music was really Lennon songs or McCartney songs, but George helped keep the cohesion because he'd put his signature parts in all of them. Unlike most guitar heroes, more often than not the whole point of George Harrison's playing was not to be noticed.

THE CLASSIC ROCK SET-UP

So you want to play rock guitar? Well you'll need a guitar and an amp. Now the first thing to remember is that these two purchases need to go together. Not all amps sound great with every guitar, and vice versa. So let's start with the guitar first.

ABOVE: *The modern electric guitar has, in general terms, developed little from the best guitars of the 1950s and 1960s, although the range of ancillary electronic effects has hugely expanded.*

Very crudely, there are three types of classic rock guitar. There's the Gibson Les Paul and SG, great riff guitars popular with hard rockers. There's the Fender Stratocaster and Telecaster, popular with bluesier players from Jimi Hendrix to Stevie Ray Vaughan. Finally there are the Rickenbackers and the Gretsches, popular with bands from the Beatles to REM who are looking for something a little twangier. If you're not sure which camp you fit into, try a few out; there's no one guitar that fits every player's style.

Next step is to choose the right amp for your guitar. If you're looking to play classic rock then you're likely to be interested in a vintage-style amp. There are three main types: Marshall style, Fender style and Vox style. Essentially what makes these amps 'vintage' is the lack of a pre-amp section to generate distortion. This means that to generate overdrive or distortion, you either have to turn them all the way up to 11 or, better, use a distortion pedal. The advantage of a pedal/vintage amp situation, especially for live work, is that you only have one volume control to worry about.

So which style of vintage amp should you go for? Well it's worth looking at what has worked for the guitar greats. The classic rock 'n' roll guitar/amp combinations are Gibson into a Marshall amp, Fender into a Fender amp and Rickenbacker or Gretsch into a Vox amp (there are of course exceptions – Hendrix, for instance, played his Fender Strat through a Marshall amp). Don't take these principles as given, however, but bear in mind that these are well tried and tested combos.

The guitar and vintage amp combo, with effects pedals as required, is the choice of most working musicians. It's simple, relatively cheap and versatile. However, if you're more confident with your sound you might want a modern style guitar amplifier like a Mesa Boogie or a Peavey Classic. These amps offer a lot more features than the vintage amps. Great if you know exactly what sound you're looking for, but confusing for a beginner. Finally, though it's between you and your ears (and the patience of the staff in your local music shop). Experiment and enjoy.

BELOW: *Prince has been at the forefront of funk guitar playing, developing the style during the 1980s with tracks such as ' When Doves Cry' and ' Purple Rain'.*

BO DIDDLEY

1928–
BAND: **SOLO ARTIST**
HEIGHT OF FAME: **1950s–60s**

Bo Diddley is one of the most influential of all rock guitar players. However, his style is not one you're going to pick up simply by reading the sheet music. With Bo Diddley's guitar playing it's all about the rhythm. This is a guitar player whose two most famous songs, 'Bo Diddley' and 'Who Do You Love', each feature only a single chord.

Bo Diddley was born in Mississippi on 30 December 1928. He was inspired to become a blues artist after seeing John Lee Hooker in action. In the early 1950s, he began working with maraca player Jerome Green, giving his music even more of a rhythmic drive, and he also signed to Chess Records of Chicago. His first single, the self-titled 'Bo Diddley' sported one of the key rock 'n' roll rhythms, one later used by Buddy Holly, the Rolling Stones and hordes of lesser-known imitators.

The extraordinarily catchy, African-derived rhythm was backed up by equally remarkable guitar playing. What Bo Diddley was doing in terms of using treble and an overdriven amplifier to create a fuzz tone was years ahead of its time, foreshadowing the likes of Jimi Hendrix. Subsequent Bo Diddley hits like 'Who Do You Love' and 'You Can't Judge A Book By The Cover' made it clear that Bo Diddley was much more than a one-trick pony. However, he will always be remembered for that one extraordinary riff-cum-rhythm played on a custom-made square-shaped guitar that looked and sounded as if it came from outer space.

RIGHT: *The great Bo Diddley poses with his custom-made guitar, notable for its peculiar shape as much as for the distinctive sound he created with it.*

AFRICAN RHYTHM – DRUM BEAT ON A GUITAR

'Bo Diddley' is a one-chord monster riff built on a rhythm that few listeners, back in the 1950s, realized actually originated in West Africa. Even Bo Diddley would have been surprised to know that.

For between Africa and Bo Diddley the rhythm had been on quite a journey. It had travelled with African slaves to Cuba where it was known as the clave, the rhythm of the bass line in Cuban song, allied to the rhumba. It can also be traced in New Orleans music too, New Orleans being the only American city in which African slaves were allowed to keep their drums, and then it made its way into African-American street culture as a rhythm known as the 'hambone'. This was used by street performers who would play out the beat by slapping and patting their arms, legs, chest and cheeks while chanting rhymes over the top of it.

As for how exactly Bo Diddley got the rhythm, it's hard to say. The man himself claims, tongue very likely in cheek, that he got it from trying to play a cowboy song by Gene Autry and messing up the beat. What he does admit to, and which is at the heart of his innovation, is that he decided to play the rhythm on the full six strings of the guitar. Thus, at a stroke, he invented a style of pure rhythm guitar playing so up front that the guitar was also effectively a lead instrument.

RIGHT: *Bo Diddley built traditional African rhythms into the heart of his music, using these to push along tracks such as 'Bo Diddley'.*

Who Do You Love?

ALBUMS: **BO DIDDLEY; BO DIDDLEY'S A TWISTER; SUPER BLUES**
SONGWRITER: **ELIAS MCDANIEL**
RECORDED: **CHESS STUDIOS**
PRODUCER: **LEONARD CHESS, PHIL CHESS, BO DIDDLEY**

Alternating between E, A and B chords is the basis of the 'Bo Diddley sound'. Experiment with dampening the strings on the fret board between the chords, but still keep the rhythm going, using the guitar in a percussive way. Generate extra rhythm by playing the full chord on the down stroke, then just clip the strings on the up stroke. Practise the rhythm on just one chord – muting then releasing. Mastering this technique will improve your rhythm playing generally.

BASIC SONG RIFF

HERE'S HOW

1. The E chord forms the basis of the riff and provides the central pulse for the rhythm. Mute and release the strings to let the sound out.

2. Use your second right finger across the top four strings at the second fret. Finally, strike all the strings open before returning to the E chord.

The key is keeping the rhythm bouncing along. Practise that unmistakable 'shuffle sound' that is produced by muting or dampening the strings.

KEITH RICHARDS

1943–
BAND: THE **ROLLING STONES**
HEIGHT OF FAME: **1960s–PRESENT**

It's easy to see Keith Richards as simply the cartoon version of the rock guitarist – the rats' nest hair, the cigarette permanently in the corner of the mouth, the bottle of Jack Daniel's perched on the amp, the 'any cooler and I'd be dead' attitude. However, important as his pose may have been to his success, one should never let it obscure the fact that he is one of the half-dozen most significant guitar players of all time in popular music. What marks him out from most of his rivals is that he is essentially a rhythm guitarist. It's not that he never plays lead, it's rather that his rhythm playing, producing classic riff after classic riff, has defined the role of the guitar in the rock 'n' roll band.

RIGHT: *Keith Richards performs an early acoustic set with the Stones. He was more typically seen playing with his electric Telecasters.*

Keith Richards was born on 18 December 1943, in Dartford, Kent, just outside London. While at art school in London he formed The Rolling Stones with childhood friend Mick Jagger. At first performing R&B and blues covers, the band really hit their stride with an original song, 'Satisfaction', based on an inordinately catchy distorted guitar riff played by Richards.

From this point on, it was the guitar riffs that would mark out the Stones' most successful songs – 'Honky Tonk Women', 'Jumping Jack Flash', 'Brown Sugar', 'Start Me Up' and others. Deceptively simple, the riffs actually owed their lasting appeal to Richards' subtle use of blues tunings – open G and open E in particular – and the habit of taking the top string off his Telecasters.

Over the years the excesses of his lifestyle have kept Richards in the headlines, but it's the intricacies of his playing that have made him a true role model for successive generations of guitar players.

FIVE-STRING TELECASTERS

In 1968 The Rolling Stones were at a watershed in their career. Their ambitious *Satanic Majesties* album had been a relative flop and they needed to revitalize their sound. Keith Richards came to the rescue with some new guitar tunings and a bunch of killer riffs, beginning with 'Jumping Jack Flash'.

Fellow guitar players were mystified as to how he got his distinctive droning sound on the lower strings. Part of the answer was in the tunings, particularly the open G. The other part lay in Keith's innovation of removing the top string from his guitars while playing in open G, and tuning the remaining strings DBGDG (high to low). Keith was so happy with the result that he began to use it constantly, using a whole range of customized five-string butterscotch Fender Telecasters, all dating from 1952 to 1954, with maple necks and black pickguards. So fond is Keith of these guitars that he gives them their own names. The best known of Richards' guitars is 'Micawber'. It has a brass replacement bridge with the nut cut to accommodate five strings, not evenly spaced across the fingerboard, but the first string moved over a little. Keith uses it live to play 'Brown Sugar' and 'Honky Tonk Women'.

His other main Telecaster is known as 'Malcolm'. The pickups and mods are the same as Micawber but this Tele stays capoed at the 4th fret and is tuned in B: BF#BD#F#. It's a little louder than Micawber and can be heard on stage for 'Tumbling Dice' and 'Jumping Jack Flash'.

RIGHT: *Keith Richards has had a long-standing love affair with the Telecaster. The Telecaster was Fender's first solid-body electric guitar, first produced in 1951.*

Jumping Jack Flash

ALBUM: **HOT ROCKS**
SONGWRITERS: **MICK JAGGER, KEITH RICHARDS**
RECORDED: **OLYMPIC SOUND STUDIOS, LONDON**
PRODUCER: **JIMMY MILLER**

This has to be one of the most famous guitar riffs of all time. It combines some great double note parts with single notes on the A and D strings. The notes on the A string can be played as a hammer-on. Practise moving between the double notes and single notes in the riff. Play big down strokes with your plectrum for the double notes, then position ready to play notes on the A and D strings.

BASIC SONG RIFF

HERE'S HOW

1 The first finger plays the B note at the 7th fret on the E string and the ring and little fingers play the A and D strings.

2 On the A string play a hammer-on between the 7th and 9th fret; practise repeating this phrase including the note on the D string.

3 Play the A note on the D string with the first finger; it forms the rest of the phrase when played straight after the hammer-on.

OPEN G TUNING

Keith Richards began experimenting with alternate tunings around 1967/68 when the Stones took a break from the non-stop touring of their early years. Keith started studying early blues guitarists, people like Blind Willie McTell and Mississippi Fred McDowell. Particular inspiration, however, came from a young American guitar player named Ry Cooder. Cooder was drafted in as a possible replacement for Brian Jones and contributed to the Stones' *Let It Bleed* album, but his most important contribution was to teach Richards the open G tuning. This involves retuning the guitar to DGDGBG. Keith refined the tuning by removing the bottom D string entirely to leave five strings tuned GDGBG. The result was a formula he succinctly summed up as 'Five strings, three notes, two fingers and an asshole, and you've got it'.

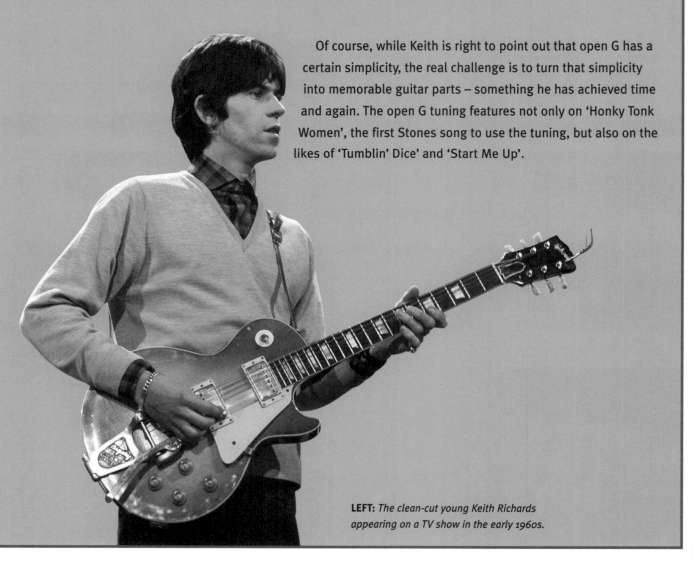

Of course, while Keith is right to point out that open G has a certain simplicity, the real challenge is to turn that simplicity into memorable guitar parts – something he has achieved time and again. The open G tuning features not only on 'Honky Tonk Women', the first Stones song to use the tuning, but also on the likes of 'Tumblin' Dice' and 'Start Me Up'.

LEFT: *The clean-cut young Keith Richards appearing on a TV show in the early 1960s.*

Brown Sugar

ALBUM: **STICKY FINGERS**
SONGWRITERS: **MICK JAGGER, KEITH RICHARDS**
RECORDED: **OLYMPIC STUDIOS, LONDON**
PRODUCER: **JIMMY MILLER**

This is a great opening riff to a great rock song. Keith Richards uses open tunings a lot and for this riff the guitar needs to be retuned to DGDGBD. The tab shows the first chords of the intro. The chords are played high up the neck so practise getting your fingering accurate. Experiment with other open tunings. Always use a guitar tuner as you'll be very likely to break strings when de-tuning.

BASIC SONG RIFF

HERE'S HOW

1 Your first finger plays the 12th fret of the G string, your middle finger plays the B string and the ring finger plays the D string.

2 This is a straight first finger across the D, G and B strings at the 12th fret. Try to only hit the fretted strings.

3 Here the first finger is back at the 9th fret of the D string and the middle finger now plays the 10th fret of the D string.

4 Simply add your ring finger to the 10th fret on the G string and keep your middle finger where it was.

LEAD OR RHYTHM?

Star guitarists almost always play lead – it's the guitar solos that allow you to show off your speed and dexterity (and pull ridiculous faces). Rhythm players, on the other hand, are generally the hardworking guys in the background who lay down the foundation for the star to solo all over. Keith Richards knows that as well as anyone, but he just doesn't care. As he says himself: 'It doesn't matter about the B.B. Kings, Eric Claptons and Mick Taylors, 'cause they do what they do – but I know they can't do what I do. They can play as many notes as there are under the sun but they just can't hold that rhythm down, baby. I know what I can do and what I can't. Everything I do is strongly based on rhythm 'cause that's what I'm best at. I've tried being a great guitar player and, like Chuck Berry, I have failed."

ABOVE: *Keith Richards is still performing with the Stones four decades after they were first formed, and shows no signs of losing his love for the electric guitar.*

Of course the joke here is that Berry and Richards between them have more or less defined rock 'n' roll guitar. After all, at its heart the music is not about fast solos or complex jazz-derived chord structures – its real foundation is the mighty riff. Guitar figures in rock 'n' roll need to anchor a song rhythmically and at the same time have a melodic component that makes them instantly memorable. Chuck Berry did it with 'Johnny B Goode' et al; Richards did it with 'Satisfaction', 'Brown Sugar' and all the rest. It is sometimes useful to remember that a great lead player playing alone is basically a showman, while a great rhythm player is rock 'n' roll incarnate.

Satisfaction

ALBUM: **BIG HITS (HIGH TIDE AND GREEN GRASS); OUT OF OUR HEADS**
SONGWRITERS: **MICK JAGGER, KEITH RICHARDS**
RECORDED: **RCA STUDIOS, HOLLYWOOD, CA**
PRODUCER: **ANDREW LOOG OLDHAM**

This is a classic Stones riff played along the A string. Use big solid notes to create that driving rock sound. You'll need to use your first finger at the B note on the A string as your middle and ring fingers will be needed at the 4th and 5th frets. Practise up and down strokes with your plectrum on the notes at the 5th fret to give you speed.

BASIC SONG RIFF

HERE'S HOW

1 The riff starts on the B note with your first finger, use down strokes here to get a good steady rhythm going.

2 Your ring finger should be waiting to hit the C# on the 4th fret of the B string. Get your little finger positioned.

3 Your little finger hits this D note – try some up and down strokes with the plectrum on these D notes at the 5th fret.

PLAYING BEHIND THE BEAT

Crucial to the process of The Rolling Stones mutating from a bunch of English kids doing their best to imitate black American blues, and then developing their own distinctive sound, was

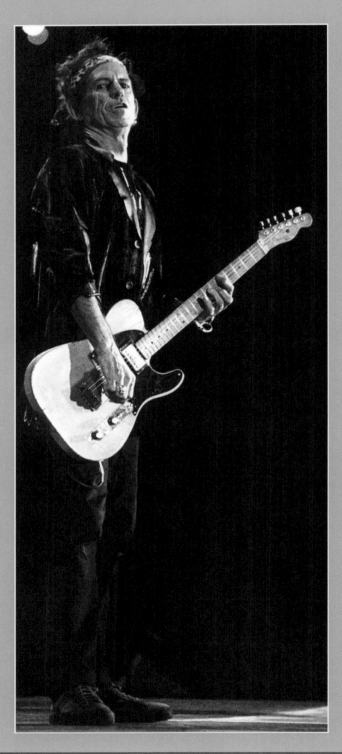

Keith Richards' determination to dig into the foundations of the blues. What he realized was that really playing the blues was not simply about playing the right notes, it was also about the notes you didn't play and, crucially, it was about rhythm and timing.

Most white blues bands strove to keep in time, but Richards watched Muddy Waters and absorbed the way in which Waters would deliberately sing and play just behind the beat, giving his music an organic looseness. That looseness was something Richards was determined to incorporate into The Rolling Stones and, in partnership with Ronnie Wood over the last 20 plus years, he has done exactly that. Sometimes that looseness can descend into sloppiness, but listen hard to Richards' guitar playing, especially on live recordings, and you can see how he will deliberately drop behind the beat during the course of a song, letting the rhythms shift and breathe. It is of course advisable to master playing in time before you start experimenting with this technique!

LEFT: *By his own admission, Richards is more of a rhythm guitarist than a soloist, although he has an acute feel for blues-oriented melodies.*

Start Me Up

ALBUM: **TATTOO YOU**
SONGWRITERS: **MICK JAGGER, KEITH RICHARDS**
RECORDED: **COMPASS POINT STUDIOS, NASSAU**
PRODUCERS: **MICK JAGGER, KEITH RICHARDS**

This song is in open G tuning. Remember that Keith Richards often plays with his bottom E string removed, so to really get that authentic Stones sound you'll have to do the same. The tuning is as it was for 'Brown Sugar'. Hit these chords hard to get a good driving rock sound. Vary your strumming technique with the plectrum and experiment with different rhythms on these big open tuned chords.

BASIC SONG RIFF

HERE'S HOW

1   We can just use the first finger across the 5th frets of G, D, G and B strings. Now get your middle and ring fingers poised ready for the next chord.

2   Use your first finger across the 5th frets of all the strings, add your middle finger to 6th fret of the B string and your ring finger will play the D string.

3   Use your first finger, this time at the 3rd fret across four strings: G, D, G and B. Be sure to place the finger in the middle of the fret to get a nice clear sound.

4   This is the same pattern two frets back. Use your first finger across three frets with your middle and ring fingers ready to come down on D and B strings.

DAVE DAVIES

1947–
BAND: **THE KINKS**
HEIGHT OF FAME: **1960s**

The Kinks, perhaps the quirkiest of all the great British bands of the 1960s, are remembered for two very different reasons. One is the quirky, typically English songwriting of Ray Davies; the other is the ferocious guitar riffing of younger brother Dave, whose influence was seminal. Many critics believe that Dave Davies' guitar riff on the band's first hit 'You Really Got Me' provided the template for what would later become heavy metal.

Dave Davies was born in Muswell Hill, London on 3 February 1947, three years after his brother Ray. In their teens, the brothers formed a rock 'n' roll group with a schoolmate of Ray's, Peter Quaife, on bass. By the summer of 1963, the group had decided to call itself the Ravens and had recruited a new drummer, Mickey Willet. Eventually, their demo tape reached Shel Talmy, an American record producer, who helped them land a contract with Pye in 1964. Before signing to the label, the Ravens replaced Willet with Mick Avory and changed their name to the Kinks. Their first two singles failed to chart, but the band's third release, 'You Really Got Me', reached number one within a month of its release. It was the first British hit to be built on a simple power-chorded guitar riff. The follow up, 'All Day and All of the Night', made number two on the charts.

Non-stop touring provoked tension in the band and Dave started releasing solo singles. Brother Ray, meanwhile, began to move away from straight-ahead rock to more unusual songs like 'Sunny Afternoon', 'Waterloo Sunset', 'Autumn Almanac' and 'Lola'. All were big hits but, by the early 1970s the band's star was on the wane. Gradually the Kinks reverted to a harder rock sound with Dave's guitar once more to the fore, and they became a popular live act in America through the late 1970s and early 1980s.

The Kinks were inducted into the Rock 'n' Roll Hall of Fame in 1990, but split up soon after. Since then, Dave Davies has released several solo albums and written his autobiography.

RIGHT: *Dave Davies performing with The Kinks on the British TV show* Supersonic *in March 1977. With his songwriting brother Ray, Davies created some of the most memorable pop riffs of the 1960s.*

THE ORIGINAL MONSTER RIFF

Ray Davies wrote 'You Really Got Me' in the front room of his parents' house with help from Dave. Ray first played the riff on a piano. Dave tried it on the guitar, and Ray shifted the tone a couple of times. Ray wanted the song to be a live showstopper and the riff to be as simple and repetitive as possible, 'like an African tribal chant,' he once said. A more obvious influence is the Kingsmen's classic 'Louie Louie,' which the Kinks used to cover.

The song was selected to be the group's make-or-break third single. The recording was a rushed, bad-tempered affair with ferocious drumming and a truly extraordinary guitar sound: fuzzed, distorted and utterly primitive. It was five years before heavy metal and twelve years before punk, but Dave Davies had anticipated both these movements in two minutes of pop revolution. In later years cynics would claim that Jimmy Page really played guitar on the song – as he did on so many 1960s pop hits – but it's hard to believe that a master craftsman like Page could ever have come up with something quite so gloriously dumb yet utterly right as the two-chord monster that is 'You Really Got Me'.

LEFT *Dave Davies, sporting a wig, in the late 1970s. Despite the changing fortunes of The Kinks as a group, their unforgettable riffs have remained ever popular. 'You Really Got Me' has been covered by many different artists including Iggy Pop and Van Halen.*

You Really Got Me

ALBUM: **KINKS**

SONGWRITER: **RAY DAVIES**

RECORDED: **IBC STUDIOS, LONDON**

PRODUCER: **SHEL TALMY**

This great Ray Davies song uses power chords to underpin the vocal line. You'll need to practise the rhythm with your strumming hand to get it absolutely right. Hit the chords hard on the down stroke and sing the verse as you play to practise your timing. Concentrate on getting a good clean hit across all the strings being held down. Listen to the record to check out the rhythm.

BASIC SONG RIFF

HERE'S HOW

1 This shows the first finger holding down the F note on the E string with the middle and little fingers holding down the A & D strings.

2 This is the same shape moved up 3 frets to the 3rd and 5th. Practise keeping the shape solid as you move around the fret board.

ELPICO – THE GREEN AMP

The ElPico was a small, green, 8–10 watt amplifier that Dave Davies found in a radio spares shop in Muswell Hill in 1962. At the time he was determined to get a dirtier, more distorted guitar sound than he could achieve with his AC30 but he couldn't afford a Watkins Dominator, which was a popular alternative at the time. Instead, he bought the little green amp and went home and started to experiment.

The ElPico had a cheap, fuzzy sound he liked, but it wasn't nearly loud enough. His first experiment involved plugging the guitar into the ElPico, the ElPico into a hi-fi amp, which was in turn plugged into a radiogram, which was finally plugged into his Vox AC30. As soon as he switched on there was a surge of electricity that sent Davies flying across the room. Clearly this was overdoing things. He simplified matters and simply plugged the ElPico into the Vox AC30. There was almost as much hum from the larger amp as there was signal from the smaller, but the tone was getting there. Still not quite satisfied, his next experiment was to slash the speaker cone of the ElPico with a razor. As it vibrated it produced a wickedly distorted sound. According to brother Ray Davies, Dave also stuck knitting needles into the speaker cone. Be that as it may, what is certain is that a sound was born. Dave Davies started using this unorthodox set-up on stage, and when it came to recording 'You Really Got Me,' there was no question what he would use...

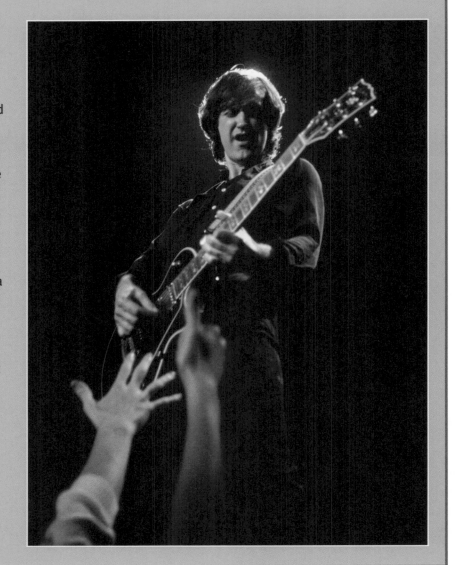

RIGHT *The Kinks were a popular live act in the United States during the early 1980s.*

All Day and All of the Night

ALBUM: **KINDA KINKS**
SONGWRITER: **RAY DAVIES**
RECORDED: **IBC STUDIOS, LONDON**
PRODUCER: **SHEL TALMY**

This is a great Kinks tune with a guitar sound that wouldn't have sounded out of place in some of the punk bands that came along around 10 or 12 years later. Again hit these chords loud and hard but practise getting the rhythm right. These shapes move around the fret board a fair bit so practise moving between each shape quickly and accurately.

BASIC SONG RIFF

HERE'S HOW

1 The first finger is on the F note on the E string, the middle and little fingers take the A & D strings, the middle finger plays the G string.

2 The same shape 2 frets up, the finger positions are exactly the same with the first finger starting at the G note on the E string.

3 Here the tab shows the same chord shape at the 6th fret, keep these shapes nice and firm and practise sliding up and down the neck.

THE MANY GUITARS OF DAVE DAVIES

Some guitar players stick with more or less the same instrument throughout their careers; others make a decisive switch, such as when Eric Clapton abandoned the Gibson Les Paul in favour of the Fender Stratocaster. Dave Davies, unusually, seems to be a man ready and willing to play whatever he can get his hands on. Here are just some of the guitars with which he has been associated.

The guitar on which he played 'You Really Got Me' was his first ever electric guitar, a 1962 Harmony Meteor. His next guitar was a 1964 Epiphone which he used on early package tours with The Hollies and the Dave Clark Five, and on the album *Kinda Kinks*. Then came a Fender Electric XII, which he used on 'I'm Not Like Everybody Else'. He also used a custom-built Guild on several of the early hits, but when it was lost in transit to the USA he went to the nearest pawnshop and bought a Gibson Flying V. He didn't find it particularly easy to play, but used it on the TV show *Shindig* because he thought it looked cool!

In the late 1960s Davies switched, like so many others, to a Fender Stratocaster, which he used a lot during the *Everybody's In Showbiz* and *Preservation* period from 1972–74. At around the same time he also played a 1952 Telecaster, which he later replaced with a 1983 Fender Elite Telecaster. In between, however, he used a 1960 Gibson Les Paul 'Gold Top'.

In more recent times Davies has returned to Fender and currently uses a sunburst 1994 Telecaster for electric work and a couple of different Ovation guitars – a Custom Legend and A Custom Balladeer – for acoustic work.

LEFT *The Kinks on the BBC TV show Shindig in 1965. Dave Davies (left) looks a little uncomfortable playing the Gibson Flying V which he had recently purchased in a local pawnbrokers.*

Tired of Waiting For You

ALBUM: **KINDA KINKS**
SONGWRITER: **RAY DAVIES**
RECORDED: **IBC STUDIOS, LONDON**
PRODUCER: **SHEL TALMY**

This is a slower Kinks tune with a wonderful melody. The tab shows the arpeggio guitar line played by Ray which complements the rocky chords played by Dave. The chords to go with the arpeggio are G and F. Try playing with another guitarist for the full effect. Practise picking out arpeggios on other riffs to vary your playing style, then slip between strummed chords and picking in the same song.

BASIC SONG RIFF

HERE'S HOW

1 The picture shows the first finger playing the B string and the middle finger playing the G string. You can try finger picking without using a plectrum.

2 For this part slide your first two fingers back 2 frets and use your little finger to play the 3rd fret of the G string.

JIMI HENDRIX

1942–1970

BAND: **THE JIMI HENDRIX EXPERIENCE**

HEIGHT OF FAME: **1960s–70s**

Just as Elvis Presley is the king of rock 'n' roll, Jimi Hendrix is the king of electric guitar. Other great guitarists have come along in his wake, but they will never match his originality. He was the first musician to understand fully the implications of a guitar's electrical possibilities. As well as playing the strings, he used effects, volume and feedback in ways that no one had ever done before. Almost everyone has copied elements of Hendrix's sound.

Hendrix was born on 27 November 1942 in Seattle, Washington. When he was 16 his father Al gave him a ukulele, and later bought him an acoustic guitar. It was clear that he had great talent, and as a young man began playing guitar for the likes of Curtis Knight, Little Richard and The Isley Brothers. By 1966 he had his own band, Jimmy James and the Blue Flames, based in New York City. There he was discovered by Chas Chandler, who brought him to England and helped him form a new band, The Jimi Hendrix Experience.

His first three singles – the incendiary 'Hey Joe', 'Purple Haze' and 'The Wind Cries Mary' – were all Top 10 hits, as was the group's first album, *Are You Experienced?* Suddenly, Hendrix was a big star. He performed at two of the seminal 1960s festivals, Monterey Pop and Woodstock; both were filmed and helped ensure Hendrix's fame. Monterey showcased his routine of burning and smashing his guitar, while at Woodstock he played an unforgettable instrumental version of 'The Star Spangled Banner'. No one had heard guitar playing like it before. Interestingly enough, Jimi's sound was achieved with quite basic equipment: he simply plugged a Fender Stratocaster into a wah wah pedal, a Fuzz Face, a Uni Vibe, or – occasionally – an Octavia, and amplified it all through a Marshall stack.

RIGHT: *Hendrix raised the status of the electric-guitar player to new heights, promoting the instrument through stunning riffs combined with outright showmanship.*

After his third album, *Electric Ladyland*, Hendrix disbanded the Experience and formed a new group, Band Of Gypsies, intending to take his music further in a jazzier direction. However, before he could fully realize his new direction, he died from choking on his own vomit after taking sleeping pills on 18 September 1970.

MARSHALL STACKS

Jimi Hendrix's guitar style, the volume he used, and his onstage pyrotechnics, demanded robust, powerful amplifiers. At first he used Vox and Fender amps, but wasn't happy with them. He then discovered the new range of high-powered guitar amps being made by London audio engineer Jim Marshall and used by The Who. Finally, he had an amp strong enough for his music. His Marshall stacks helped shape his heavily overdriven sound, and, above all, gave him the opportunity to use feedback as a musical effect. Of course, Jimi's patronage soon meant that the Marshall amp was the only one for any new rock band to be seen with.

All of which was a triumph for Jim Marshall, the man behind the amp. A former drummer, he'd

PYROTECHNICS

An essential part of what made Jimi Hendrix the enduring star he is was his showmanship. Before Hendrix rock guitar heroes were mostly studious musicianly types like Eric Clapton, whose idea of showmanship was to close their eyes during a solo. Hendrix came out of a different world, that of soul and blues, where artists were expected to have a stage act.

So British audiences gazed on in amazement when Hendrix performed tricks like playing the guitar with his teeth or behind his head; when he set it on fire they could scarcely believe their eyes. Here was not just another guy who could play the guitar well, but a fully-fledged entertainer.

This talent for showmanship also manifested itself in Hendrix's playing, with his extravagant use of effects to make his guitar sound that much more bizarre than anything anyone had heard before. It's an approach that reached its apotheosis in the classic footage from Woodstock of Hendrix playing 'The Star Spangled Banner.' Here Hendrix ran through the full gamut of his effects pedals – the UniVibe, Octavia, Cry Baby and Fuzz Face, plus copious feedback – first one at a time and then all together, to create an extraordinary array of noises evoking the sounds of the Vietnam War, such as machine-gun fire and bombs dropping. Here Hendrix demonstrated that showmanship and pyrotechnics were not trivial distractions, but vital parts of a guitarist's armoury.

LEFT: *Hendrix pushed guitar playing to its absolute limits both in terms of tonal quality and melodic experimentation, all using his 'left-handed' Stratocasters.*

Hey Joe

ALBUM: **ARE YOU EXPERIENCED**
SONGWRITER: **BILLY ROBERTS**
RECORDED: **OLYMPIC STUDIOS, LONDON**
PRODUCER: **CHAS CHANDLER**

This is the part of the song where the guitar and bass play a climbing scale. It comes in just after Hendrix takes the main solo. Use your first three fingers and play nice big chunky notes. Listening to the record will help you improve your timing on this section. Use this song to practise climbing riffs on the bass strings of your guitar. Try to play along with the band.

BASIC SONG RIFF

HERE'S HOW

1 The riff starts on the C note on the 3rd fret of the A string. Use your ring finger to play this note and hold it firm.

2 This is the start of the ascending climb along the A string from the 2nd fret to the 5th. Once you've played this, play the same frets on the E string.

3 Here we go back to the A string to play an ascending scale from the 4th fret to the 6th fret. Use all fingers here.

4 The riff finishes with this E7#9 chord – known as the Hendrix chord because he used it so often.

LEFT-HANDED STRAT

Thanks to Jimi Hendrix, the Stratocaster is the biggest-selling electric guitar in history. Before Hendrix, most top guitar players in the UK used Gibsons and Rickenbackers. After he appeared, almost all of the leading guitarists, including Jeff Beck and Clapton, switched to the Stratocaster.

ABOVE: *Hendrix in action with his Strat.*

Hendrix bought his first Strat from Manny's Music in New York, in 1966. The left-handed Hendrix bought right-handed Strats because he preferred to have the controls on top. This set-up created a totally different tension to the standard feel of the guitar. Also out of its usual position was the patented Fender tremolo arm which enabled him to bend notes and entire chords without the guitar going out of tune. The Strat's low action and narrow neck were also ideally suited to Hendrix's style as, he had very large hands to start off with, and he was able to fret across all six strings with the top joint of his thumb alone.

Despite Hendrix owning dozens of Strats at one time or another, only six are still known to be in circulation. The best known of these is the white 1968 Strat that Hendrix played at Woodstock, which was resold in 1993 for £750,000. It is now on display at the Experience Music Project in Seattle, built by Microsoft billionaire Paul Allen, a Hendrix fan.

opened his own London music shop in 1960. His customers often asked for louder amplifiers, so Marshall started making them himself, having enlisted the help of Ken Bran, an electrical technician and former customer. They built a prototype and immediately received orders for 50 more. By 1964 Marshall Amplifiers had their own factory in west London. Among their customers was Pete Townshend of the Who, who asked for a still more powerful amp. In response to this request, the company developed the first 100-Watt amps. Townshend also asked for a larger 8x12 cabinet for the speakers. The impracticality of this cabinet led to a 'stacked' version, one 4x12 on top of another. The Marshall stack was born, and it only needed Hendrix to take it to the next level.

FUZZ BOXES

A fuzz box is essentially a unit designed to increase the instrument's volume, while simultaneously increasing the 'overdriven' quality of the tone – to give it the 'fuzz' if you like. It allows the guitar to sustain and feed back with the touch of a button. Hendrix started using a fuzz box, the Maestro Fuzz Tone, almost as soon as they became available, while playing with Curtis Knight. On moving to London he found a new favourite, The Fuzz Face. This was originally manufactured by Arbiter and sported a distinctive round shape inspired by a microphone-stand base. Hendrix used the device a great deal, though as the sound of a fuzz box so closely resembles that of an overdriven amplifier it is not always easy to detect its use on record.

Later on, Hendrix acquired a personal effects guru, Roger Mayer, who built a variety of custom effects units for him, including the Octavia. This was a unique combination of fuzz box and octave doubler. It produces a sound that is an octave higher than the note that the guitarist is playing, as well as creating some otherworldly noises all its own. Hendrix can be heard using the Octavia on songs such as 'Purple Haze'.

All Along the Watchtower

ALBUM: **ELECTRIC LADYLAND**
SONGWRITER: **BOB DYLAN**
RECORDED: **RECORD PLANT, NEW YORK**
PRODUCER: **JIMI HENDRIX**

A great Jimi Hendrix lead solo from the intro of 'All Along the Watchtower'. This solo uses some great bends to express the melody. It's amazing how much feeling Hendrix managed to squeeze into so few notes. Use bending techniques to really let those high notes scream. Practise pulling some big bends after coming off a run to get more melody from your lead solos.

BASIC SONG RIFF

HERE'S HOW

1. Start on the G# at the 13th fret of the G string with the middle finger, this allows your first finger to play the B string.

2. This is the bend up from the 14th fret of the B string, use your ring finger to pull a nice big bend here.

3. This shows a down pull on the G string at the 11th fret; again use your ring finger to get maximum downward pull on the string.

4. The last note of the riff is a bend at the 12th fret on the B string. Use all your fingers to support the bend.

JIMMY PAGE

1944–
BAND: **THE YARDBIRDS; LED ZEPPELIN**
HEIGHT OF FAME: **1970s**

Often thought of as simply the prototypical heavy-metal axe hero – all monster riffs and epic solos – Jimmy Page is actually one of the most versatile guitarists to appear during the rock era. He was a renowned session man before emerging as an artist in his own right and, even within his work with Led Zeppelin, he incorporated subtle acoustic playing and modal experimentation, not to mention playing with a violin bow, alongside the familiar heroics.

Jimmy Page was born in London in January 1944. He started playing guitar aged 12, inspired by Elvis' guitarist Scotty Moore. In his teens he toured with rock 'n' roll band Neil Christian and the Crusaders, before giving up music temporarily in favour of painting. He soon returned to guitar playing, however, and during the 1960s established himself as Britain's number one session guitarist, playing on records by everyone from The Kinks to The Rolling Stones, before finally agreeing to join The Yardbirds, where he briefly formed a partnership with fellow guitar legend Jeff Beck. Following The Yardbirds' split, he formed Led Zeppelin and moved, once and for all, to centre stage.

With Led Zeppelin Page was able to show off his entire box of tricks, whether creating archetypal heavy metal riffs like 'Whole Lotta Love', mystical but still thunderous modal riffs like 'Kashmir', or delicate acoustic constructions like 'Black Mountain Side', where he first revealed the influence of folk guitar great Bert Jansch. Then, with 'Stairway To Heaven', he put it all together to create a rock epic that started out with acoustic delicacy and then built to a majestic electric climax. It's the ultimate guitar anthem, and learning to play it is a rite of passage for budding guitar players (though one discouraged by guitar shop employees worldwide, who tire of hearing it being mangled by novices).

RIGHT: *Jimmy Page here seen with his trademark Gibson twin-neck guitar. One neck had 12 strings, the other six.*

ROGER MAYER FUZZ BOX

Back in 1964, when Jimmy Page was a young session guitarist, his friend Roger Mayer was working for the British Admiralty in the field of vibration and acoustic research, to aid with underwater warfare. Jimmy Page was already interested in stretching the sonic capabilities of his electric guitar and he encouraged Mayer to build him an effects unit. The result was one of the first ever fuzz boxes, featuring germanium transistors.

The unique sound was an immediate hit. Producers clamoured for Page to use the effect on records they were making – for instance the fuzz guitar on the 'Who's 'My Generation' was played by Page rather then Pete Townshend. Popular demand soon meant that Mayer made further units for the other great studio guitarists of the time, Jeff Beck and Big Jim Sullivan, who used it on pop hits like 'Hold Me' by P.J. Proby, which may have contributed to the effect becoming seen as essentially a novelty. Mayer went on to build more sophisticated fuzz boxes that would become part of Jimi Hendrix' signature sound. Page, however, still believed in the potential of the original box, and when he started making his own music with Led Zeppelin, its true potential was unleashed.

BELOW: *Jimmy Page with the band that made him famous, Led Zeppelin. Zeppelin remain one of the biggest selling rock bands in history.*

Whole Lotta Love

ALBUM: **LED ZEPPELIN II**
SONGWRITERS: **JIMMY PAGE, ROBERT PLANT, JOHN BONHAM, JOHN PAUL JONES, WILLIE DIXON**
RECORDED: **OLYMPIC STUDIOS, LONDON**
PRODUCERS: **PETER GRANT, JIMMY PAGE**

Also known as the theme to BBC TV's weekly chart show Top of the Pops, *this is one of the most famous rock riffs ever. The key to getting it right is in the rhythm; the fret board finger movement is minimal but you will need to get the rhythm right. Practise playing single heavy notes on the bass strings and sliding into the chord at the 7th and 8th frets.*

BASIC SONG RIFF

P.M = Palm Muting

HERE'S HOW

1 This shows the ring finger at the 7th fret of the E string, your first finger will be back at the 5th fret of the A string.

2 Practise this part of the riff, rocking between the E and A strings. Get the timing right before moving to the next chord.

3 Slide into this chord to complete the riff, first finger on the A string and ring and little fingers on the D and G strings.

THE VIOLIN BOW

At the heart of *The Song Remains The Same*, the epic concert and fantasy film capturing Led Zep in their pomp and splendour, is a 28-minute version of 'Dazed And Confused', a showcase for Page's amazing guitar skills. At the song's dramatic highpoint Page brings out a violin bow and uses it on his Les Paul, coaxing out some quite extraordinary sounds.

Though an undeniably effective piece of showmanship, the use of the violin bow was more than a simple stunt. Page first recorded with a violin bow while still with The Yardbirds, and used it regularly on record with Led Zep. He didn't simply bow the guitar either, but combined it with wah wah and echo. As for where he got the inspiration for it, accounts differ. Page claimed that the idea was put to him by a classical string player while he was doing studio work. Others, however, have pointed out that Eddie Phillips, guitarist with another 1960s band, The Creation, used the bow before Page. Whatever the truth of it, if you're thinking of trying this yourself a key tip is to make sure you put rosin on the bow, as the rosin sticks to the string and makes it vibrate.

RIGHT: *The violin bow and the guitar are not a typical combination, but Jimmy Page used them together to create eerie musical effects.*

THE GIBSON DOUBLENECK

When it came to live work Jimmy Page's versatility provided some logistical problems – most obviously on 'Stairway To Heaven'. On record the song began with Page playing a Martin Acoustic, then he switched to a Fender XII 12-string for the rockier section, while the solo was played on a Fender Telecaster. Clearly, switching guitar repeatedly in the course of single song wasn't an option, yet the song, an instant classic, demanded to be played live. Then Page came up with a solution. He remembered that Gibson had briefly produced a twin neck guitar in the late 1950s. The Gibson EDS 1275 had one neck with twelve strings and another with six, both using the same body.

LEFT: *Jimmy Page was a true showman. He is still heavily involved in music, and has remastered the Zep back catalogue.*

Heartbreaker

ALBUM: **LED ZEPPELIN II**
SONGWRITERS: **ROBERT PLANT, JIMMY PAGE, JOHN PAUL JONES, JOHN BONHAM**
RECORDED: **A&R STUDIOS, NEW YORK**
PRODUCERS: **PETER GRANT, JIMMY PAGE**

This is another great Led Zeppelin rock riff all on the bass strings to get a nice heavy sound. The riff starts with a bend at the G note on the E string before falling into the main riff. There are some quick notes on the A string in the second part. Practise changing pace from the faster double notes to the main notes in the riff, and use up and down strokes with the plectrum to get speed.

BASIC SONG RIFF

HERE'S HOW

1 This is the bend on the E string. Use your ring finger here then drop down to the A string for the next part of the riff.

2 Hit the open A then bring your ring finger down on the C note at the 3rd fret of the A string.

3 This three-note run is on the D string. Play open then use your first and middle fingers to play the 1st and 2nd frets.

The guitar was out of production, but Page custom ordered one from Gibson. Now he was able to perform the crucial sound change, midway through 'Stairway', live with just one guitar. Soon afterwards other 1970s guitar heroes, including Steve Howe of Yes and jazz-rock supremo John McLaughlin, ordered their own doublenecks. However, it wasn't simply the live convenience that interested Page. He noticed that if you leave the 12-string neck switched on and play on the six-string neck, the 12-strings start vibrating in sympathy to produce an Indian sitar-like effect.

MAESTRO ECHOPLEX

Jimmy Page is one of the great pioneers when it comes to electric guitar effects. His role in developing the fuzz box is only the most influential example.

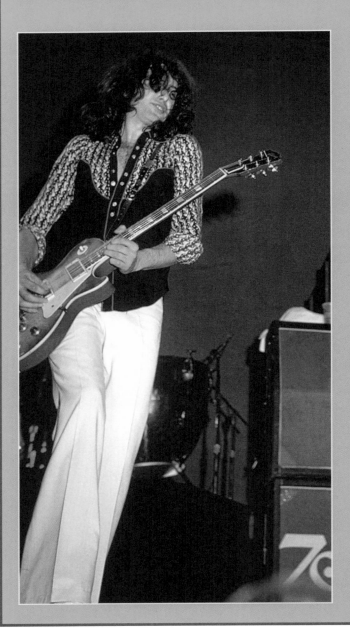

Similarly innovative was his championing of the Maestro Echoplex. This was a mid 1970s solid-state circuitry tape-based echo machine. Essentially the guitar part went on the machine, was recorded on tape, and played back a fraction of a second later to provide an echo. Jimmy Page used the straightforward echo effect a lot, but his urge to experiment also unearthed new possibilities in the machine. He would play a note or even a chord, clean or with edge, and give it a long delay rate, then he'd add the sustain which made the echo repeat, and adjust the frequency so that the echoes sped up like a plane taking off, before reaching an almighty crescendo. It's an effect he used to breathtaking effect on 'Whole Lotta Love', and which was crucial in establishing the Led Zep sound as more powerful than anything previously heard. Modern digital effects units can, of course, offer far longer lasting and infinitely tweakable echoes, but purists will assure you that they can never match the analogue warmth of the original Echoplex.

LEFT: *Here Page is playing with a sunburst Gibson Les Paul. Page tended to use his double-necked guitar only in stage performances rather than during recordings.*

Kashmir

ALBUM: **PHYSICAL GRAFFITI**

SONGWRITERS: **ROBERT PLANT, JIMMY PAGE, JOHN BONHAM**

RECORDED: **STARGROVES; OLYMPIC STUDIOS, LONDON**

PRODUCER: **JIMMY PAGE**

This is a great driving Jimmy Page riff that runs up the fret board. To play this riff, tune the bottom E string down to a D – check that it's in tune by comparing it with the open D string. Make sure you include the bottom D in this riff for maximum effect. Listen to the record to practise the rhythm. Practise using and varying up and down strokes with the plectrum to achieve that stuttering sound on the rhythm guitar.

BASIC SONG RIFF

1   The tab picture shows the first finger at the 12th fret on the A string. Remember you only need to hit the bottom two strings.

2   By adding the middle finger at the 13th fret of the A string we start the ascending riff. Work on your up and down strokes, you'll soon get that great rhythm.

3   This is a two-fret jump up to the 17th fret, it's easiest to slide the little finger up to here. Remember to take care detuning and tuning your strings.

Stairway to Heaven

ALBUM: **LED ZEPPELIN IV**
SONGWRITERS: **ROBERT PLANT, JIMMY PAGE**
RECORDED: **ISLAND STUDIOS, LONDON**
PRODUCER: **ANDY JOHNS**

The tab shows the lovely arpeggio pattern at the start of 'Stairway to Heaven'. It does require some practice, but it is rewarding to play once you've nailed it – this is why it's such a popular practice tune in guitar shops around the world. It's probably best to only play this one at home! Split each section of the tab to practise until you are comfortable, then put them all together.

BASIC SONG RIFF

1. Your first finger covers all 5th fret notes on the G, B and E strings whilst your ring finger plays the 7th fret of the D string.

2. Keep your first finger in position, but now your little finger plays the E string and your middle finger plays the 6th fret of the D string.

3. Still keep your first finger in position but here your little finger plays the 8th fret of the E string. Follow the tab closely.

4. The first finger is on the G string, middle finger on the E string and the ring finger is on the B string.

Famous Albums

Led Zeppelin's first four albums were officially untitled. They are usually known as Led Zeppelin I, II, III *and* IV, *although the latter is also referred to as 'Four Symbols.' Six Zeppelin albums appear in the listing of the top selling albums of the 1970s, with Led Zeppelin IV selling a remarkable 22 million copies in the United States alone.*

ALBUM: **LED ZEPPELIN II**
YEAR: **1969**
RECORDED AT: **OLYMPIC, LONDON**
PRODUCED BY: **JIMMY PAGE**

ALBUM: **LED ZEPPELIN III**
YEAR: **1970**
RECORDED AT: **HENLEY GRANGE**
PRODUCED BY: **JIMMY PAGE**

ALBUM: **LED ZEPPELIN IV**
YEAR: **1971**
RECORDED AT: **HENLEY GRANGE**
PRODUCED BY: **JIMMY PAGE**

5 First finger is at the 1st fret of the B string, the middle finger is at the 2nd fret of the G string and the ring finger is at 3rd fret of the D string.

6 The final shape is the middle finger on the 2nd fret of the D string and the ring finger on the 2nd fret of the G string.

BAND INFO

LED ZEPPELIN

BAND FORMED: **1968**

ALBUMS: **12 including reissues**

TOTAL ALBUM SALES: **more than 40 million**

ORIGINAL LINE-UP

LEAD: **ROBERT PLANT**

GUITAR: **JIMMY PAGE**

BASS: **JOHN PAUL JONES**

DRUMMER: **JOHN BONHAM**

THE ALLMAN BROTHERS

1946–1971 AND 1943–
GUITARISTS: **DUANE ALLMAN, DICKEY BETTS**
HEIGHT OF FAME: **LATE 1960s–EARLY 1970s**

Most bands would be happy to have one great guitarist in their ranks. The Allman Brothers were lucky enough, for a time, to have two, Duane Allman and Dickey Betts.

In the late 1960s Duane Allman was already a highly rated session player who had appeared on a whole range of Atlantic soul classics. Determined, however, to make his own music, he put a band together with his brother Greg on vocals and organ, Dickey Betts on joint lead guitar, Berry Oakley on bass, plus both Butch Trucks and Jaimoe Johanson on drums. They combined a love of R&B and rock 'n' roll with the improvising ability of a top-flight jazz group, and their incendiary live shows soon won then a devoted following.

They hit their stride with their second album, 1970's *Idlewild South*, which added a softer acoustic texture to their music and included the classics 'Midnight Rider' and 'In Memory of Elizabeth Reed', an instrumental tribute to Miles Davis, written by Betts.

In March 1971, the band, always at their best on stage, recorded a live album, *At Fillmore East*, which became an instant classic.

Duane Allman, meanwhile, took time out to moonlight with Eric Clapton's Derek & The Dominoes project, contributing the lead riff and classic slide guitar part to 'Layla'. Then, in October 1971, tragedy struck as he was killed in a motorcycle accident. The Allmans had been midway through work on their next album, *Eat A Peach*, at the time. They completed it as a five-piece, with Dickey Betts playing all of the lead and slide guitar parts. This was their first album to reach the Top 10.

From then on Betts and Greg Allman shared leadership of the band, with Betts writing and singing the group's biggest hit, 'Ramblin' Man', and the instrumental classic 'Jessica'. The Allmans split up in 1976, and after several abortive reunions came back together properly in 1989.

RIGHT: *Duane Allman was a true guitar hero who achieved legendary status in only two years of performing, before his untimely death in 1971.*

THE CORICIDIN BOTTLENECK

Guitar players have used the necks from glass bottles since slide guitar playing began, back in the early days of the blues. However, only Duane Allman has been identified with one particular brand of bottle. This was the Coricidin bottle. Coricidin was a cold medicine and Allman happened to have a cold and to be taking the medicine just at the time he started to learn to play slide. He then discovered that this particular medicine bottle just happened to be the perfect size and length to fit on most people's second or third fingers, and to be just about exactly the width of a standard-issue Les Paul electric guitar's neck.

BELOW: *Duane Allman created a haunting blues sound with his Gibson Les Paul, accentuating the vocals while also pushing the guitar to the front of the track.*

Allman's use of the Coricidin bottle soon became legendary and slide guitar players eagerly sought them out, but in the late 1970s the glass bottles were banned under federal child-proofing regulations. The new plastic bottles were safer for kids, but no bargain for slide guitar aficionados who had come to depend on the resonance and sustain achievable with Coricidin bottles, and found themselves paying up to 20 dollars apiece (in 1975 dollars) for original bottles scavenged from the back of medicine cabinets.

Demand grew to such a point that in 1985, one Scott 'Blue' Bernstein worked on producing a replica, and soon started making them commercially for the exclusive use of guitarists who want to play slide. So although you can still use broken-off bottlenecks, metal ratchets and specially-made plastic and glass slides, the Coricidin bottle will probably be around for a while to come.

Jessica

ALBUM: **BROTHERS AND SISTERS**
SONGWRITER: **FORREST RICHARD BETTS**
RECORDED: **CAPRICORN SOUND STUDIOS, GA**
PRODUCER: **JOHNNY SANDLIN**

A nice acoustic guitar intro. The riff starts with an open A before going into the A chord. Listen to the recorded version to help with the rhythm. Use up and down strokes with the plectrum and practise moving between the G bass note and the chord shape. Try to make the chords play out clearly and avoid touching the open strings with your fretting fingers.

BASIC SONG RIFF

HERE'S HOW

1. This picture shows the A shape. This can be played with the first finger across the D,G and B strings at the 2nd fret.

2. Here the middle finger plays the G at the 3rd fret of the bottom E. Practise moving back and forth between this note and the next chord.

3. In this picture the first finger plays the G string, the middle finger plays the B string and the ring finger plays the D string.

PETE TOWNSHEND

1945–
BAND: **THE WHO**
HEIGHT OF FAME: **1960s–70s**

Pete Townshend is up there with Keith Richards as one of the all time great rock rhythm-guitar players. Unlike most rock bands, The Who based their rhythm on Townshend's guitar, letting drummer Keith Moon and bassist John Entwistle improvise over his foundation, while singer Daltrey belted out his vocals. That formula gave their records a unique power and momentum, while in live performances Townshend took the band into even wilder sonic territory with his fondness for ending songs in a flat-out cacophony of noise as he destroyed his guitars on stage.

He was born Peter Dennis Blandford Townshend on 19 May 1945 in Chiswick, London, England, the son of singer Betty Dennis and saxophonist Cliff Townshend. In his teens he started playing banjo in a Dixieland jazz band, before joining The Detours as rhythm guitarist, alongside Roger Daltrey and John Entwistle. Soon the Detours evolved into The Who, and a string of classic Townshend compositions like 'I Can't Explain', 'My Generation' and 'Substitute' established the group not just as a great rock band, but one that explicitly confronted the turmoil of the times.

Townshend's song writing became ever more complex, leading to the rock opera *Tommy*, before switching to a simpler, but still blisteringly effective, hard-rock style for the classic albums *Who's Next* and *Live At Leeds*. During the 1970s Townshend began to develop a solo career but the resulting, more personal, material never gained the mass audience that the band continued to enjoy, boosted by the live film *The Kids Are All Right* and the feature films based on the rock operas *Tommy* and *Quadrophenia*. In recent years

RIGHT: *Pete Townshend's on-stage guitar demolitions with The Who have sometimes distracted attention from his formidable talents as a rock musician.*

Townshend has been heavily involved in writing books and working on an epic multimedia work called *Lifehouse.*

GUITAR SMASHING

The first time Pete Townshend smashed a guitar on stage was during an autumn 1964 Who gig at north London's Railway Tavern. During the show Pete Townshend repeatedly smacked his Rickenbacker against the ceiling while trying to shake off some feedback whistles. The band's fans loved it, and they dared him to abuse his guitar again for the band's second set. 'The guitar broke,' Townshend recalled, 'and the audience was waiting for me to sob over it — like, "Hey, that'll teach you to jump around like a lunatic."' However, Townshend decided to act as if the destruction had been deliberate. 'So I smashed up the guitar even more and jumped all over the bits, which gave me a fantastic buzz.' The crowd, of course, went wild. Unfortunately, from then on fans expected The Who to destroy their gear at every gig – a situation that at one time threatened to drive the group into bankruptcy, especially as their fortunes dipped after the huge success of their first few singles. However, the success of *Tommy* later gave Townshend the financial leeway to destroy as many guitars as he liked (and drummer Keith Moon the opportunity to drive as many Rolls Royces into swimming pools as he wanted!).

GIBSON SG

The Gibson SG is the model of guitar with which Townshend is most associated. He used this model almost exclusively on stage between 1968 and 1973. He tended to use SGs dating between 1966 and 1970, which are identified by their full black wraparound pickguard.

In fact, when Gibson changed the SG's specification in 1971, it caused Townshend major upset. In an interview with *Guitar Player* magazine in 1972 he confided that 'They took the old SG off the market like about a year ago, so we used up every old SG in the country...I raided every music store in the country practically, looking for old SGs.' This was of course a particular problem for Townshend, with his penchant for destroying his guitars at the end of gigs. So when supplies of 1966–1970 models did finally dry up, he then briefly switched to pre-1966 models. As well as the classic red SGs he also appears to have owned at least two, or possibly three, Polaris White Gibson SG Specials. Then, at the end of 1973, he switched permanently to using a Gibson Les Paul Deluxe.

Recently, though, Gibson have introduced a Pete Townshend-endorsed Gibson SG. According to Gibson, Townshend's SG possessed 'the most recognizable Gibson electric guitar style of the 1960s.' The new Signature model is a replica of that guitar, with its bold, pointed horns, a Townshend signature decal on the back of the peghead and a Pete Townshend Signature SG hardshell case. Townshend himself has commented that 'This guitar is amazing. It looks, sounds, and feels exactly like the SG I used during *Live At Leeds*.'

ABOVE *Townshend playing one of his favourite Gibson SG guitars.*

Pinball Wizard

ALBUM: **TOMMY**
SONGWRITER: **PETE TOWNSHEND**
RECORDED: **IBC STUDIOS, LONDON**
PRODUCERS: **CHRIS STAMP, KIT LAMBERT**

This song has some great big power chords to practise your 'windmill swings' with your strumming arm ! The tab shows the main guitar riff as chords. Practise your timing with these chords it has to be spot on if you're to come even close to sounding like Pete Townshend from The Who. Play these chords big and loud using only down strokes with the plectrum, and listen to the song to help you with timing.

BASIC SONG RIFF

HERE'S HOW

1. Your first finger plays the B note on the A string; ring and little fingers play the F# and B notes on the D and G strings.

2. Let your first finger slide down to cover the second frets on the D and G strings, remember to include the open A in this chord.

3. Use your first finger on the 2nd fret of the G string and ring finger on the 3rd fret of the B string. Note the open D string this time.

4. The riff finishes with this E5 chord; use your middle finger at the second fret on the A string and your ring finger at the second fret on the D string.

59

JERRY GARCIA

1942–1995
BAND: THE **GRATEFUL DEAD**
HEIGHT OF FAME: **1960s–70s**

Jerry Garcia is a guitarist who spans the extremes. On the one hand he's famous for epic electric-guitar solos, improvising around classic Grateful Dead tunes like 'Dark Star' for anything up to an hour. On the other hand he's also known for tight, focused acoustic playing on his trusty Martin Dreadnought, as featured on the two definitive Dead studio albums *Workingman's Dead* and *American Beauty*.

He's also the man who played perhaps the first pedal steel-guitar solo rock fans had ever heard – when he guested on CSNY's classic 'Teach Your Children'. All this despite having a mutilated right hand – he lost his right middle finger just below the first knuckle while chopping wood in his youth.

Jerry Garcia was born in San Francisco on 1 August 1942. He learned to play guitar when he was 15 years old, originally playing folk and rock 'n' roll. He dropped out of school aged 16 and spent a brief time in the army. After leaving the military he moved to Palo Alto where he met future Dead lyricist Robert Hunter. Garcia bought a banjo and began playing in local bluegrass bands. One of these, Mother McCree's Uptown Jug Champions, eventually evolved into the Grateful Dead in 1966, with Garcia switching to electric guitar.

Jerry Garcia's electric-guitar playing incorporated aspects of a whole range of music: bluegrass and Chuck Berry, country & western, and modern jazz could all be heard in the mix. During the band's early years Garcia played a Guild, then an assortment of Gibsons, mainly Les Pauls, plus the occasional Strat. From the late 1970s onwards, however, he mostly played custom-made guitars. For many years, these were made for him by Doug Irwin. One, nicknamed 'Tiger', was to remain Garcia's main instrument for an unprecedented

RIGHT: *Jerry Garcia was a true legend of American guitar playing. On his death in 1995 President Bill Clinton remembered Garcia as 'an American icon'.*

11 years. In the 1990s he also used guitars made by a remarkably talented novice guitar maker named Stephen Cripe.

The Grateful Dead, with their combination of roots influences and psychedelic sensibilities, became a colourful American institution and a massive live draw right up until 1995 when Garcia's hard living finally caught up with him and he died of a heart attack while attending a drug rehabilitation clinic.

GUITAR VERSUS BANJO

'I put my first real energy in music into the five-string banjos,' said Garcia. "I slowed the records down and painstakingly listened to every lick and worked them out. Having gone through that process with banjo, when I went to electric guitar I knew how to learn it.'

Garcia had actually started out by playing a Danelectro electric guitar during his mid teens. However. by 1960 he was caught up in the folk and bluegrass revival of the time and switched his instrumental focus to the more traditional banjo. He soon mastered the basic techniques of bluegrass banjo, playing clawhammer and two-finger picking, and at first took an orthodox approach, trying to sound as much as possible like an old-time Kentucky mountain picker. All that changed though with the influence of Bill Keith, who, through his work with Bill Monroe, revolutionized bluegrass banjo. Keith used dazzling 'chromatics' (melodic arpeggios, strings of notes or 'runs' up and down the musical scale) and new chordal complexity. Garcia was immediately inspired by Keith's playing. He appreciated and extended Keith's subtle rhythmic accents, and in particular he worked on learning Keith's mastery of the whole of the fretboard, often playing higher notes on a lower string, and using this facility to produce arpeggiated passages that swooped dramatically up and down the neck. Garcia particularly liked producing long ascending lines in this fashion. All of this exerted an obvious influence when, from 1964 onwards, Garcia turned his attention back to the electric guitar.

LEFT: *Garcia brought together multiple musical influences, from heavy rock to gentle folk tunes.*

Dark Star

ALBUM: **LIVE DEAD**

SONGWRITERS: **JERRY GARCIA, ROBERT HUNTER**

RECORDED: **THE FILLMORE WEST; AVALON BALLROOM, SAN FRANCISCO**

PRODUCERS: **THE GRATEFUL DEAD**

This is a lovely riff to improvise over from The Grateful Dead, the masters of rock improvisation. The tab shows the riff starting on the G string, but once you've mastered the tune fingering it sounds good anywhere on the guitar. Experiment with some bends to add expression to the tune. It's a fairly slow riff so it's a good time to practise some up and down strokes with the plectrum.

BASIC SONG RIFF

HERE'S HOW

1. Try the first part of the riff with your middle finger on the 4th fret of the G string; get used to dropping down to the B string for that D note.

2. Here you can use your first finger to play the 3rd fret on the G string. Split the riff into sections and repeat them.

3. The first finger is playing the D note at the 3rd fret of the B string. Experiment with the riff and improvise playing some of your own notes.

DOUG IRWIN GUITARS

During the early 1970s Garcia became increasingly dissatisfied with mass-produced guitars. In 1972 he came across a guitar maker from Sonoma, California, called Doug Irwin, who had just made his first electric guitar (known as 001). Garcia bought it for $850 and ordered another one custom-made. In May 1973 he received the custom–made guitar, known as 'Wolf', for which he paid $1500. He gave Irwin's 001 to original Dead road crew member Ramrod. Wolf sported a maple neck, 24-fret ebony fingerboard, a blonde Western 'quilted' maple body and a core made from purpleheart. Its electronics were broadly similar to a Strat but with an Alembic Stratoblaster installed.

At the same time Irwin delivered Wolf, Garcia commissioned another guitar and told him time and money were no object. Irwin evidently took him at his word, as he spent seven years making the new guitar. However, the effort was well worth it as the new guitar, christened 'Tiger', became Garcia's main axe from 1979 right up to 1990. Tiger was an unusually heavy 6kg (13$\frac{1}{2}$lb) guitar with a pearl coverplate, an ebony fingerboard on maple neck, an arched cocobola top and back, vermilion neck and body striping, and a flamed-maple body core.

Garcia's final Doug Irwin guitar took an epic 11 years to make. Delivered in 1990 it was nicknamed Rosebud (after the inlaid dancing skeleton on the ebony cover plate) and cost $11,000. Irwin saw it as his masterpiece, a beautifully made electric guitar that also doubled as a guitar synthesizer, with MIDI controls built in. It is almost a twin of Tiger, but is lighter at 5.2kg (11$\frac{1}{2}$lb), as its core had been hollowed out to house a gutted out Roland GK-2 guitar synthesizer interface. It soon replaced Tiger as Garcia's regular guitar.

LEFT *Jerry Garcia crafting an extended solo on Tiger during a 1988 concert. The guitar was christened Tiger because of the inlay on the battery/preamp compartment cover.*

St. Stephen

ALBUM: **AOXOMOXOA**

SONGWRITERS: **JERRY GARCIA, ROBERT HUNTER, PHIL LESH**

RECORDED: **PACIFIC RECORDERS, CA**

PRODUCERS: **THE GRATEFUL DEAD**

This is a gentle lead guitar intro. The sound is a lovely mix of jazzy improvisation and rock that was a trademark of the band. All the notes are around the top end of the neck and around the top three strings. Try improvising with other notes around this area of the guitar neck – see what happens when you start to trust your own ear.

BASIC SONG RIFF

HERE'S HOW

1. This shows the ring finger at the 11th fret kicking off the solo. The other fingers are well placed behind to play notes on the lower frets.

2. Play this note at the 9th fret of the B string with your first finger leaving your middle and ring finger free. Play gently.

3. For this note let your middle finger drop down to the E string to play the D note at the 10th fret.

JEFF BECK

1944–
BAND: **YARDBIRDS**
HEIGHT OF FAME: **1960s**

Jeff Beck is the guitarists' guitarist par excellence. He may not be a household name like his contemporaries Eric Clapton and Jimmy Page, but ask any of the greats and they'll tell you that when he's on there's no one to touch Jeff Beck. He's a man who makes the electric guitar do the apparently impossible. The secret is the extent to which he plays the entire guitar: using his fingers instead of a guitar pick for greater speed and control over the fretboard, Beck adds constant twists of the volume and tone knobs to shape the notes as he's playing them, and then further bends the sounds with his expert use of the whammy bar.

Beck was born in Wallington, England, on 24 June 1944, just before the end of World War II. He took up the guitar in his teens, inspired as much by jazz as rock. A fast learner, he was soon in demand as a session player, before he replaced Eric Clapton as the Yardbirds' lead guitarist in 1965. Beck's innovative style on hits like 'Heart Full of Soul' and 'Shapes of Things' helped influence the psychedelic sound of the 1960s.

In 1967 he formed The Jeff Beck Group, releasing two albums which ploughed a similar furrow to early Led Zeppelin, though with rather less commercial success. Increasingly impatient with the rock format, Beck switched gears in 1975 with the groundbreaking instrumental jazz-fusion album *Blow By Blow*, which surprisingly became the biggest hit of his career. Produced by Sir George Martin, the album fused the complexity of progressive rock with jazz and thus opened up the horizon for future guitar instrumentalists like Steve Vai and Joe Satriani.

RIGHT: *Jeff Beck was a true innovator on the electric guitar. He not only experimented with style but also with sound, being one of the earliest exponents of distortion.*

THE WHAMMY BAR

The whammy bar or tremolo arm is a very powerful sound-altering tool for the guitar. As a string bending vibrato unit it actually physically changes the sound the guitar makes as it is played rather than simple transforming the sound after the fact. The development of the whammy bar goes back to the early 1950s when a cumbersome unit called the Bigsby was developed for the Epiphone ES-295, and used by Scotty Moore. The first integral whammy bar came with Leo Fender's 1954 introduction of the Stratocaster. Initially it was intended to be a tool to add some slight vibrato to single notes and chords.

It was only in the mid 1960s that guitarists started fully to experiment with its possibilities. Jimi Hendrix was perhaps the most flamboyant proponent of the whammy bar (just listen to his version of 'The Star Spangled Banner'), but it is Jeff Beck that most thoroughly explored its capabilities. Beck managed to play whole melodies using only the whammy bar and would even combine finger- and bar-vibrato, thereby shaping the notes in remarkable ways, sometimes even creating an almost human voice. His early work on the whammy bar was all the more extraordinary when you realize that these early units tended to make the guitar go out of tune very quickly.

In the late 1970s, Floyd Rose came up with a double locking system which largely solved the tuning problems and has allowed guitar virtuosos (and Beck disciples) like Steve Vai and Joe Satriani to conjure extraordinary effects from the whammy bar. See Steve Vai's appearance in the movie *Crossroads* for an awesome demonstration of the technique.

LEFT: *Jeff Beck can truly make a guitar sing, and the whammy bar is just one tool in his box of tricks.*

I Ain't Superstitious

ALBUM: **TRUTH**

SONGWRITER: **WILLIE DIXON**

RECORDED: **ABBEY ROAD STUDIOS, LONDON**

PRODUCER: **MICKIE MOST**

A great blues riff that uses nice thick and solid notes on the bass strings. Starting off on the 8th fret of the A string the riff moves to a nice alternating pattern on the D string before finishing with double notes at the 3rd fret on the A and D string. Play these notes slow and hard to give you that heavy blues sound. Practise the alternating notes on the D string.

BASIC SONG RIFF

swing

HERE'S HOW

1 It sounds great if you use your ring finger to slide into this F note on the A string just before you play it out.

2 This alternating part rocks between the 6th and 8th frets; use your first and ring fingers for these notes. Tap a beat with your foot to keep time.

3 Back at the 3rd fret on the A and D strings, use your middle and ring fingers to hold the C and F notes. Keep the whole riff steady.

THE TELE-GIB

Jeff Beck's most unusual guitar was the so-called Tele-Gib, built for him by noted guitar maker and pickup specialist Seymour Duncan. In 1974 Duncan was working in the repairs and modifications section of the Fender Soundhouse. After watching Beck play, Duncan had the notion that what Beck needed was a guitar that played like a Fender but which had the tone of a Les Paul. As no such instrument existed Duncan set out to make one. He began with the carcass of a 1959 Fender, gave it a new maple fingerboard and cut the fret slots by hand, before putting in Gibson Les Paul frets. Then he went through the tortuous job of rewinding a broken pair of old Gibson 1959 humbuckers. The pickups came from an old 1959 Gibson Flying V that once belonged to Lonnie Mack. The finishing touches included a lever switch knob from an old telephone switchboard, while the volume and tone control knobs and control plate are from an early 50's Telecaster. Jeff liked the instrument immediately and used the 'Tele-Gib' on the seminal *Blow By Blow* album, which included arguably the finest Beck guitar performance, on 'Cause We've Ended As Lovers'.

RIGHT: *Crafted by Seymour Duncan, the Tele-Gib guitar was a unique fusion of Fender and Les Paul. This is a copy of Jeff Beck's guitar, also made by Duncan.*

Where Were You?

ALBUM: **GUITAR SHOP**
SONGWRITERS: **JEFF BECK, TERRY BOZZIO, TONY HYMAS**
RECORDED: **THE SOL STUDIO, ENGLAND**
PRODUCERS: **JEFF BECK, TERRY BOZZIO, TONY HYMAS, LEIF MASES**

This riff is all played along the the B string using the first, middle, ring and little finger. This is great for practising moving up and down the fret board on one string and improving accuracy in your lead playing. Try to get fluency between notes with all your fingers. Get used to climbing the fret board using one finger after another, then descend using the same technique.

BASIC SONG RIFF

HERE'S HOW

1 The tab shows the first finger playing the C# note at the 14th fret with the ring finger about to play the F# at the 17th fret.

2 Simply slide the first finger up one fret to the D, again use your ring finger to play the F# at the 17th fret.

3 This is a lovely descending passage that you can play between the 17th and 12th frets. Try using different fingers to find which suits you best.

MARC BOLAN

1947–1977
BAND: TYRANNOSAURUS REX, T REX
HEIGHT OF FAME: **1970s**

Marc Bolan, lead singer and guitarist with T Rex, was one of the original glam rock stars. For a couple of years during the early seventies, T Rex were greeted by the wildest scenes of mass hysteria since Beatlemania. And while Marc is more often thought of as a lead vocalist and songwriter, it's his distinctive way with a guitar riff, played on his signature white Stratocaster, that underpinned the band's hit singles – pop classics like 'Get It On' and 'Telegram Sam'.

RIGHT: *During the early 1970s, Marc Bolan's appearances on TV shows such as the BBC TV chart rundown* Top of the Pops *helped to promote his image as a teen icon and glam rock superstar.*

Although he appeared to many to be an overnight sensation, Marc Bolan had actually been around the pop scene for a while before his time finally came. He was born Mark Feld in Hackney, East London, on 30th September 1947. Leaving school at 14, Bolan went on to form his first band, Suzie And The Hula-Hoops, in 1959.

After recording some early demos, Bolan signed to Decca Records as a solo artist in August 1965. A song called 'The Wizard' was released as a single, but failed to chart. The follow-up singles met a similar fate. Then, after a brief stint in a band called John's Children, Bolan formed his own band, Tyrannosaurus Rex, in July 1967. The band released several psychedelic folk-tinged albums, attracting a firm fan in DJ John Peel and scoring a minor hit with 'Deborah', but still remaining a cult act.

All that changed in 1970 when the band changed their name to the catchier T Rex and released a single, 'Ride A White Swan'. This saw them switching to a tighter, poppier sound, underpinned by Marc's switch to electric guitar. Hit single followed hit single for the next two years. Unfortunately, however, from 1974 onwards their popularity nosedived, and three years later Marc Bolan died in a car accident. Yet today, while many of his contemporaries are forgotten, Marc Bolan's string of hit singles remain classics of riff-based pop-rock.

BOLAN'S WHITE FENDER STRATOCASTER

The guitar with which Marc Bolan is most closely associated is undoubtedly his white late-'60s Fender Stratocaster. He actually had two of these guitars, one of them marked out by a teardrop-shaped paisley enamelled sticker on the upper body horn. He bought the first of the guitars in 1969 and used it on his next album *Beard Of Stars*, released in March 1970. It is rumoured that 'Ride a White Swan', the single that finally launched him into the big time, was actually a tribute to his beloved white Strat.

BELOW: *Bolan performs on a T Rex Christmas TV special in December 1972. Note the enamelled teardrop sticker on his white Stratocaster.*

Bolan was a friend of Eric Clapton during the late 1960s, so it's more than likely that it was Clapton's example that persuaded him to buy a Strat. Bolan's Stratocaster sound, though, is distinctively his own. In part this is due to his use of the capo. On some of his earlier songs, the capo can be seen as high as the sixth or even seventh fret, giving the guitar an almost mandolin-like sound. He also preferred to fingerpick rather than use a plectrum. According to Bolan's long-time producer, the legendary Tony Visconti, one of Marc's two white Stratocasters was given to David Bowie after they'd done a TV show together, just weeks before Bolan's death. The other, sadly, was stolen when his house was burgled shortly after he died.

Get it On

ALBUM: **ACOUSTIC WARRIOR**
SONGWRITER: **MARC BOLAN**
RECORDED: **WALLY HEIDER, LOS ANGELES, CA; ADVISION, LONDON; TRIDENT, LONDON**
PRODUCER: **TONY VISCONTI**

Also known as 'Bang a Gong (Get it On)' this song starts with a great boogie riff in E at the 2nd fret of the A string. Listen to the record to get the rhythm exactly right. Practise playing the C# note at the 4th fret with your ring or little finger, keep your index in position at the 2nd fret of the A string. Try this same shape and movement on the D string, then come back to E.

BASIC SONG RIFF

HERE'S HOW

1 Use your index finger to play the B note at the 2nd fret of the A string, then use your middle or ring finger to play the alternating note at the 4th fret of the A string.

2 This shows the C# note being played at the 4th fret of the A string, practise your rhythm playing with this riff to get that classic T Rex boogie feel.

THE DALLAS RANGEMASTER

The British-built Dallas Rangemaster was an effects pedal that Marc Bolan used frequently. This was an early example of a booster unit, designed to give a treble boost to the dark British amps of the time.

Demand for such a unit had grown as the guitar began to figure as a lead instrument, rather than as just part of the rhythm section. The Rangemaster supplied a new, punchier sound. This kind of booster pedal is subtly different to a distortion pedal, although it does not offer an altogether clean boost, but modifies the sound quite a bit. It excites certain frequencies and pushes the amp to allow it to create rich tube distortion. The pedal gives the tone a crunchy overdrive and warms it thanks to the use of germanium transistors.

One classic early use of the Rangemaster was on the epochal John Mayall and the Bluesbreakers album. On that record, Eric Clapton famously used the Les Paul and Marshall amp combination. Less well known is that on several of the tracks his sound was boosted by the use of a Dallas Rangemaster. The original Rangemaster was not a pedal at all, but a tabletop unit with just an on/off switch and a volume knob.

Clapton's example inspired many other guitarist to experiment with the Rangemaster: Brian May used a modified version on nearly all his guitar parts with Queen, which is how he got such a distinctive tone out of his Red Special through walls of AC30s.

Early heavy metal guitarists were particular fans of the unit. Ritchie Blackmore of Deep Purple used it often, and another key user was Tony Iommi of Black Sabbath. He used the Rangemaster to boost the signal from his Gibson SGs into his Laney amps, and created what is perhaps the definitive heavy metal guitar sound.

RIGHT: *As an artist, Bolan appeared to both the older fans who appreciated his earlier, more mystical material, as well as new listeners attracted by the poppy riffs of tracks like ' Twentieth Century Boy'.*

Ride a White Swan

ALBUM: **VARIOUS COMPILATIONS**
SONGWRITER: **MARC BOLAN**
RECORDED: **N/A**
PRODUCER: **TONY VISCONTI**

This is a nice lead riff that plays under the rhythm at the start of the song. Pick out these notes individually and remember to use hammer ons between the notes at the 4th and 6th frets. Try playing with the record to get your lead playing locked in with the rhythm. Playing this lick is good practice for playing between bass and high strings and will improve your lead playing generally.

BASIC SONG RIFF

HERE'S HOW

1 The first part of the riff shows the index finger playing the 4th fret of the D string and the hammer on with the ring or little finger at the 6th fret.

2 Bring your index finger down to the A flat note at the 4th fret of the top E to play the next part of the riff, let this note ring out.

3 Finally use your index finger to play the 4th fret of the B string and your ring or little finger to hammer on to the 6th fret of the B string.

JAMES TAYLOR

1948–
BAND: **SOLO ARTIST**
HEIGHT OF FAME: **LATE 1960S–EARLY 1970S**

James Taylor invented the modern day singer-songwriter genre: the introspective balladeers with just an acoustic guitar for company. There had been singers accompanying themselves on the guitar before, of course, but generally they'd been out-and-out folk singers in the Woody Guthrie tradition.

What James Taylor did was to take the instrumental style of the folksinger and turn it inwards, rejecting protest songs in favour of love songs. With 'Fire and Rain' and 'Sweet Baby James', Taylor succeeded in soundtracking the lives and loves of the post-Woodstock early 1970s generation. While it's his classic songwriting and smooth voice that are the first things most people associate with James Taylor, his fingerpicked acoustic accompaniments have also been an enormous influence on generations of guitar-playing songwriters.

James Taylor was born 12 March 1948 in Boston, the second son of a wealthy, musical family. Later the family moved to Chapel Hill, North Carolina, where James' father was dean of the medical school. Taylor studied cello as a child, but first took up the guitar when he was 12. After suffering teenage stints at boarding school and in a psychiatric hospital following a bout of depression, he moved to Greenwich Village where he started performing.

His first break came when he was signed to The Beatles' Apple label in 1968. His big breakthrough came with his second album *Sweet Baby James* released on Warners in 1969. Since then, his musical career has never looked back. Album after album has gone gold or platinum with his *Greatest Hits* collection selling over 10 million copies. He continues to sell records consistently, having discovered the knack of growing old gracefully.

RIGHT: *James Taylor is a master of intricate blues and rock melodies, and his fingerpicking style makes him difficult to imitate.*

JAMES TAYLOR'S GUITAR STYLE

James Taylor's guitar playing is all about fingerpicking, He scarcely ever plays block chords. Instead he uses complex right-hand picking patterns with distinctive bass lines picked out with his thumb.

His style is based on the classic Merle Travis two fingers and thumb picking style, though over the years he's customized it considerably and always uses three fingers instead of two. Unlike many fingerpickers, Taylor doesn't use a thumb-pick either. Instead he simply grows his thumbnails along with the rest of his fingernails, though while he keeps his other nails about an eighth of an inch beyond the tip of the finger, he grows the thumbnail a little longer and files it straight across rather then curved around the line of the quick. In this way, it acts more like a thumbpick. Such is Taylor's aversion to picks that if he breaks a nail he'll glue on an artificial nail rather than use a pick.

Thankfully while Taylor's right-hand work is deceptively complex and difficult to imitate, his left-hand work is relatively straightforward. He almost always uses standard tuning, with the occasional excursion into G (DGDGBD), and with particular fondness for open chords (especially since an accident resulted in him severing a nerve in his left index finger, thus making chord barring difficult). Taylor relies heavily on the capo, sometimes even using different capo positions within a single song. 'One, Your Smiling Face' actually has three separate capo positions so when playing it live the capo would start on the second fret, move to the fourth and end up on the sixth. Asked why he used the capo so much, the endearingly modest Taylor once commented, 'It's really the thing that shows how rudimentary a player I am.'

BELOW: *James Taylor delivers an acoustic set. Taylor's favoured acoustic is the Olsen SJ.*

You've Got a Friend

ALBUM: **MUD SLIDE SLIM & THE BLUE HORIZON**
SONGWRITER: **CAROLE KING**
RECORDED: **CRYSTAL STUDIOS, HOLLYWOOD, CA**
PRODUCER: **PETER ASHER**

For this song we've used a capo on the 2nd fret to bring the tuning up a tone. This tune sounds lovely strummed or picked-finger style on an acoustic guitar. Move gently between chords for a nice relaxed feel and experiment mixing strumming with finger style. Try a capo on other songs to find the key that suits you best. Practise picking arpeggios on other chords.

BASIC SONG CHORDS

Capo 2nd fret

HERE'S HOW

1 Use your middle, ring and little fingers to keep your first finger free for the 1st fret on the B string in the next chord.

2 This picture shows a C chord shape. Notice the little finger playing the G note on the E string; this gives the chord a lovely melodic ring.

3 Play this chord by using the first, middle and little finger on the E string. Practise using your little finger on other chords.

JAMES TAYLOR'S OLSON SJ

In his early days, James Taylor favoured Gibson guitars, using a J-50 on much of his material. Then John McLaughlin introduced him to a luthier named Mark Whitebook who made him a series of acoustic guitars, modelled on the Martin dreadnought style and generally equipped with Takamine pickups.

However, Whitebook retired from the guitar-building business and since 1989 Taylor has found himself a new luthier, Minnesota guitar-maker James Olson. Olson left a guitar in James Taylor's dressing room, when he was playing a gig locally, and Taylor called him the next day.

Taylor loved the guitar, but he wanted a non-cutaway version with the same neck dimensions. Taylor took the cutaway guitar on the spot with the understanding that he would exchange it when the new guitar was completed. Once the new guitar was finished, however, Taylor decided to keep the cutaway guitar as well, and while he was at it, he ordered an Olson dreadnought to round out his collection. All three guitars remain active in Taylor's stage setup, but he considers the SJ to be his main instrument and has used it on every CD he's recorded since he purchased it.

For the SJ, Olson decided to use East Indian rosewood on the guitar's back and sides. It sports an abalone rosette and purfling, but simple fingerboard inlays give it an understated look. The only thing different about James Taylor's personal SJ from Olson's standard design is that the guitar's neck is laminated using rosewood instead of mahogany. Taylor had the guitar set up with an L.R. Baggs LB-6 pickup and John Pearse strings.

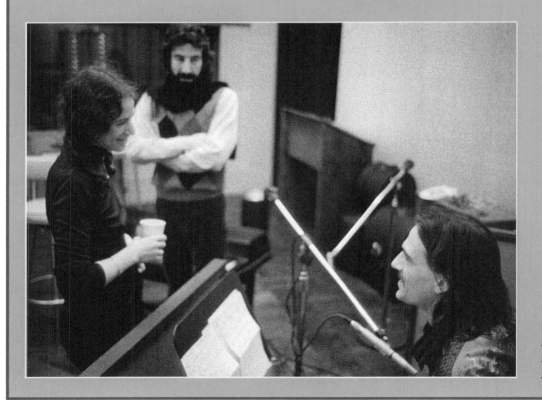

LEFT: *James Taylor and Carole King had a close working relationship, collaborating on several projects.*

Sweet Baby James

ALBUM: **SWEET BABY JAMES**
SONGWRITER: **JAMES TAYLOR**
RECORDED: **SUNSET SOUND STUDIOS, LOS ANGELES**
PRODUCER: **PETER ASHER**

These are the main chords used in James Taylor's classic 'Sweet Baby James'. Get used to moving between different chords fluently, and don't be afraid to experiment by adding or taking away a note here and there. Use a nice relaxed strumming style on an acoustic guitar for this tune. Practise moving between these chords fluently and integrate them into your repertoire. Try singing along as you play.

BASIC SONG CHORDS

G

Em^7

A^{7}sus^4

HERE'S HOW

1 Use your first finger for the B note at fret 2 of the A string. Your middle finger should play the G note on the top E string.

2 For this chord cascade your fingers down the fret board from first to little to play the four notes shown on the chord diagram. Keep G open.

3 Your middle finger plays the E note on the D string, ring and little finger will play the B and E string at the 3rd fret.

CARLOS SANTANA

1947–
BAND: **SANTANA BLUES BAND**
HEIGHT OF FAME: **1970s–PRESENT**

Carlos Santana is the most purely melodic of the great rock guitarists. His controlled, fluid technique makes a uniquely smooth ride, as in his classic interpretation of 'Black Magic Woman' or his huge recent hit, the aptly titled 'Smooth'. At other times, he uses it to keep the listener engaged while he works through some exceedingly complex jazz rock – as on the John Coltrane-inspired duo album he made with fellow guitar legend John McLaughlin, *Love Devotion Surrender*.

Carlos Santana was born on 20 July 1947 in Autlan De Navarro, Mexico where he spent his early years. His father was a mariachi violinist and Carlos took up the violin at five, but at eight switched to the guitar. Later the family moved to Tijuana, where he began playing in clubs and bars. Then, in the early 1960s, the family moved to San Francisco where he finished high school in 1965. The following year he formed The Santana Blues Band, a collective of Bay Area musicians. While nominally a blues band, it stood out from the competition by incorporating elements of Latin music and jazz into its sound. Soon they were signed to Columbia Records and released their first album in 1969. It became an instant hit following the band's performance at Woodstock, and proved the template for several more hit albums, peaking with 1970's *Abraxas*.

This album showed the full range of Santana's abilities. The material mixed rock, jazz, salsa and blues, but whether the band were playing salsa tunes like 'Oye Como Va', Latin-flavoured jazz-rock as on 'Samba Pa Ti', or moody blues-rock with their classic version of Fleetwood Mac's 'Black Magic Woman', what kept things together was the utterly distinctive sound and tone of Carlos Santana's lead guitar.

RIGHT: *Carlos Santana is the archetype of the smooth Latin guitar sound, although his musical influences stretch well beyond indigenous Latin-American music.*

THE RED GUITAR

During the 1970s the electric-guitar market had more or less boiled down to a war between the two big players, Gibson and Fender. These two big manufacturers made a fine job of producing mass-market guitars, but for players looking for something classier, but without wanting to pay the fortune needed for a fully custom-made guitar, there wasn't much choice out there. Then along came Paul Reed Smith. A young man with a vision, he started manufacturing guitars in his attic in Annapolis, Maryland. He produced several prototypes and did his best to talk visiting musicians into trying them out. The first person to take him seriously was Carlos Santana, who was thrilled with the extraordinary attention to detail and overall quality of Smith's guitars. His endorsement helped Smith set up PRS guitars as an increasingly flourishing business at the high end of the market.

Santana himself has had any number of PRS guitars over the years, but his clear favourite is the so-called Red Guitar made in the original PRS factory in Annapolis. It sports a Brazilian rosewood neck and mahogany body plus an East Coast Curly Maple top. You can see its photo on the back of Santana's multi-platinum *Supernatural* album.

There are also several Santana-endorsed PRS models available to the general public – just don't expect them to feature Smith's private stash of Brazilian rosewood. PRS also supply Santana-endorsed pickups carefully designed to offer devotees the chance to recreate Santana's signature smoothness of sound.

RIGHT: *The Red Guitar is a beautiful instrument from PRS guitars, made from the finest rosewood, mahogany and maple. It is easy to see why it is Santana's favourite guitar.*

She's Not There

ALBUM: **MOONFLOWER**
SONGWRITER: **ROD ARGENT**
RECORDED: **CBS STUDIOS, SAN FRANCISCO, CA**
PRODUCER: **CARLOS SANTANA**

This is a great little repetitive riff played over four strings. You can try up and down strokes with the plectrum on this one to vary the speed of the riff. Try to move easily between the different strings to give the riff a nice fluid sound. Listen to the song to check your timing. Once you feel relaxed and confident playing this riff use a few slides into the notes to accentuate the melody.

BASIC SONG RIFF

HERE'S HOW

1 The ring finger plays the 5th fret of the D string and the first finger is back to play the 3rd fret of the G string.

2 Here the first finger has dropped down to the B string to play the D note on the 3rd fret.

3 Bring the ring finger up to play the C note which is at the 5th fret of the G string.

Famous Albums

The Santana Band's debut self-titled album was among the bigger splashes made by San Francisco's second wave of acid rock artists, buoyed by the group's incendiary live shows, including Woodstock. Abraxas features two of Santana's better known tracks, 'Black Magic Woman' and 'Oye Como Va', while Supernatural saw Carlos Santana top the charts a remarkable 29 years later.

ALBUM: **SANTANA**
YEAR: **1969**
RECORDED: **PACIFIC RECORDING, CA**
PRODUCERS: **SANTANA**

ALBUM: **ABRAXAS**
YEAR: **1970**
RECORDED: **PACIFIC RECORDING, CA**
PRODUCERS: **SANTANA**

ALBUM: **SUPERNATURAL**
YEAR: **1999**
RECORDED: **FANTASY STUDIOS, CA**
PRODUCERS: **SANTANA**

RIGHT: *Carlos Santana is still going strong. To date he has sold over 50 million albums and in concert he had entertained nearly 30 million fans.*

BAND INFO

THE SANTANA BAND
BAND FORMED: **1966**
ALBUMS: **36**
TOTAL ALBUM SALES:
50 MILLION

ORIGINAL LINE-UP
LEAD: **CARLOS SANTANA**
KEYBOARDS: **GREGG ROLIE**
BASS: **GUS RODRIGUES**
VOCALS: **GREGG ROLIE**
DRUMMER: **ROD HARPER**
More than 60 musicians have played with the band since 1966

Smooth

ALBUM: **SUPERNATURAL**

SONGWRITERS: **ROB THOMAS, ITAAL SHUR**

RECORDED: **FANTASY RECORDING STUDIOS, BERKELEY, CA**

PRODUCERS: **CARLOS SANTANA, CLIVE DAVIS**

The higher up the neck you go the more narrow the distance between each fret. Playing riffs high up the neck will get you used to the differences in fret width. You may need to slightly adjust your body position when moving between high and low frets, find out what position is most comfortable for you. Use hammer-on technique with first and ring finger for this riff. First finger can cover notes at the 12th fret.

BASIC SONG RIFF

HERE'S HOW

1 Try to make the hammer-on sound smooth by holding the original note firm with the first finger and hitting the 14th fret with the ring finger.

2 Use the first finger on the B string and make sure your ring finger is poised ready to hit the A note at the 14th fret of the G string.

3 Practise moving between the high strings down to the bass strings. Use your first finger to play the D ocatve at the 12th fret of the D string.

RITCHIE BLACKMORE

1945–
BAND: **DEEP PURPLE, RAINBOW**
HEIGHT OF FAME: **1970s**

Ritchie Blackmore is the epitome of the heavy-rock guitar god – a mean, moody Strat-slinger dressed in black. His claim to fame may be having written the ultimate rock guitar riff in 'Smoke on the Water', but his real importance as a guitarist lies in the way he incorporated classical and even country influences into his playing to create a heavy-rock style. This style is entirely original, and sounds quite different from that purveyed by blues-oriented guitarists such as Clapton and Hendrix.

Blackmore was born on 14 April 1945, in Weston-super-Mare, UK. His first guitar was a Framus, a Spanish guitar made in Germany. He took classical guitar lessons for a while, but the influence of rock 'n' roll soon convinced him to trade up to an electric. His early influences included Duane Eddy, Big Jim Sullivan – Britain's premier session guitar player during the 1960s – and Hank Marvin, who fronted legendary '60s British group The Shadows. The real turning point, though, was his discovery of country pickers like Chet Atkins. He was amazed by the speed and dexterity of Atkins' playing and started to practise for eight hours a day in order to acquire quick-picking and double-note riffing techniques that form the bedrock of his style to this day.

Ritchie played with several groups during his early teens. He left school when he was 15, worked as an apprentice radio mechanic at nearby London Airport, and then played with Screaming Lord Sutch. By the time he reached 16, his devotion to and subsequent mastery of fast, complex riffing led to plenty of session work, often sharing studio dates with Jimmy Page. Finally, in March 1968, Blackmore became a founder member of Deep Purple.

RIGHT: *With Deep Purple Ritchie Blackmore pioneered the heavy metal sound, combining powerhouse rhythms with the nimblest of solos and melodies.*

At first the band played psychedelic pop, but with the addition of new vocalist Ian Gillan they soon became hard rockers, providing a new generation with monster riffs like 'Black Night'. Blackmore once described the song as 'A total rip-off. I stole the riff from Ricky Nelson's record of "Summertime".' Another classic was 'Smoke On The Water', written after the band went to see Frank Zappa playing in Montreux and the venue caught fire.

AIWA TAPE DECK

Ritchie's best known effects unit is the Aiwa open-reel tape deck used both in the studio and live, which acts as an echo unit and a preamp. He introduced the Aiwa on the 1974 Burn tour. The tape deck was originally intended to act as a delay unit, as the use of open-reel tape decks for echo was a fairly common technique at the time. Mike Oldfield notably used an Akai open-reel machine

ENGL AMPS

For many years Blackmore played his guitars – first the Gibson then the Fender Strat – through Marshall amplifiers. He even persuaded Jim Marshall to build him a custom amp, alleged to be the most powerful Marshall amplifier ever made. Most guitarists might have been satisfied with that, but Blackmore is a restless soul, and was still not entirely happy.

He felt the sound only worked at full volume; anything less and he thought it sounded thin. He compensated for this perceived deficiency by using his Akai tape deck preamp which fattened up the mid-range sound, but he still felt a lurking dissatisfaction. Then, in the early 1990s, while playing some smaller club dates, he tried out a German made Engl amplifier, which used the traditional tube valve technology, and was amazed to realize that he'd

found the amplifier of his dreams. This was a huge boost to the small German company founded in the 1980s. Since then they've gone on to produce a Ritchie Blackmore signature model based on a classic, proven design also equipped with a number of innovative features. For instance, you can vary the amount of crunch for the two channels Clean and Lead via the Gain-Boost switch. Also, each of the two Gain stages (Lo and Hi) is equipped with a dedicated master volume control, or you can activate Master A and Master B via footswitch.

LEFT: *Richie Blackmore had a long journey to find his ideal amp system, discovering it in the Engl tube valve amp.*

Smoke On The Water

ALBUM: **MACHINE HEAD**
SONGWRITERS: **IAN GILLAN, RITCHIE BLACKMORE, IAN PAICE, JON LORD, ROGER GLOVER**
RECORDED: **MONTREUX CASINO, THE GRAND HOTEL, SWITZERLAND**
PRODUCERS: **DEEP PURPLE**

These are fantastic power chords frequently used in heavy-metal tunes. Like the 12-bar chords in rock 'n' roll, you can move these shapes around the fret board to hear echoes of many great rock songs. Crank the amp up to '11' and enjoy! Power chords need to be very solid; learn to slide them up and down the fret board. Use the sliding sound to accentuate the tune.

BASIC SONG RIFF

HERE'S HOW

1 Use your first, ring and little finger on this shape. The basic shape stays the same throughout. Keep the chord rigid as you move up and down.

2 This is the shape up five frets from the first shape. Try to include the slide as part of the riff, and experiment with different rhythms with your plectrum.

3 The shape is now at the 8th fret; from here use the sound sliding down to the 7th fret as part of the tune.

WAH WAH

The wah-wah pedal is the gizmo that created the 'wakka wakka' effect beloved of Jimi Hendrix and most early 1970s guitarists. Ritchie Blackmore was at the forefront of this sound, though it has become somewhat less fashionable now.

ABOVE: *An array of pedals beneath a guitarist's feet can be more of a distraction than an asset, but Ritchie Blackmore used his sounds only to enhance the piece being played.*

The first wah-type sounds could be found on country albums in the late 1950s and early 1960s. However, these were not obtained by a separate effects unit but simply by the player working the tone knob. Vox was the first company to have commercial success with the Wah. It came about accidentally, when testing an oscillator for an amp. The sound created brought people running to find out what on earth the effect was, and Vox knew they were on to a winner.

Soon afterwards Vox introduced the classic Cry Baby Wah to the US market and guitar playing was never quite the same again. Over the next few years Vox also tried different variations on the wah theme, such as the bass wah and the fuzz wah. A legion of imitators also sprang up. By the late 1960s there were probably 40 or 50 different manufactures making wah-wah pedals on both sides of the Atlantic. Some of the more familiar names were Marshall, DeArmond, Sound City, Colorsound, Gibson, Fender, Gretsch and Kay. Many of these devices offered extra sounds like fuzz, sirens, surf, tornado, etc. As the late 1970s approached, the wah effect was becoming unhip, and the number of manufacturers dropped accordingly. To hear definitive use of the wah-wah in a hard-rock setting, listen to Ritchie Blackmore's playing on *Deep Purple In Rock*.

on *Tubular Bells*. The echo effect comes from the delay between the record head and the playback head with the recorder in monitor mode to produce a delay. If the deck can do it, plug the guitar in and set the left channel to monitor the recorded signal and the right channel to the original signal. The faster the tape is run, the shorter the echo/delay. However, as Blackmore discovered, these open-reel tape decks with valve electronics can be used as guitar preamps as well an echo units. Lindsey Buckingham used a Sony tape deck as a preamp with Fleetwood Mac. At various times Ritchie used both effects. The preamp he used to give his sound an altogether fuzzier effect. Having tried it successfully in the recording studio, he decided to use it on stage as well and the Aiwa tape deck has become a familiar sight to anyone who has been fortunate to see Blackmore play live over the subsequent 30 years. He plugs the Aiwa in between his guitar and the amp and uses a foot pedal to control how much effect it has.

Black Night

ALBUM: **DEEP PURPLE IN ROCK**

SONGWRITERS: **IAN GILLAN, RITCHIE BLACKMORE, IAN PAICE, JON LORD, ROGER GLOVER**

RECORDED AT: **N/A**

PRODUCED BY: **DEEP PURPLE**

This tab shows the riff picked out on the bass strings – this gives a great heavy metal sound. Use your first and ring finger to hit the notes on the fret board. Practise moving between the three bass strings (E, A and D). Play slowly then speed up once you feel comfortable. Alternate use of first and ring finger, and get used to moving between bass strings. Every note in this riff counts, so play them solidly.

BASIC SONG RIFF

HERE'S HOW

1. Use muting to cut notes off before playing the next one. This technique will help to accentuate heavy-metal riffs. Use it on other songs.

2. Drop down to the D string with your first finger; with practice you'll be able to move easily between these notes that are only two frets apart.

3. Your ring finger should play this note on the E string, every note should sound loud and bold, remember the guitar and bass lead the band on this riff.

RIGHT: *Ritchie Blackmore became one of the most recognizable figures of Deep Purple, proving how much the status of lead guitarists had changed since the 1950s. He would, however, have an emotionally troubled relationship with other band members and finally left in 1994.*

Since You've Been Gone

ALBUM: **DOWN TO EARTH (RAINBOW)**
WRITTEN BY: **RUSS BALLARD**
RECORDED AT: **LE CHATEAU, PARIS, FRANCE**
PRODUCED BY: **ROGER GLOVER**

This tune uses some nice big power chords at the intro – notice again the two-fret distance between the notes to give that solid power chord sound. Practise using up and down strumming techniques to create interesting rhythm patterns. You'll need to get comfortable moving these shapes around the fret board. Use big down strokes with the plectrum for power and combine with up strokes to vary the rhythm.

BASIC SONG RIFF

HERE'S HOW

1 This chord uses the first finger to play the B and E strings, so you'll need to stretch your ring and little fingers to play the A and D strings.

2 Change shape here, your first finger plays the D note on the A string and your ring and little finger plays the D and G strings.

3 Move this whole shape up two frets to the 7th and 9th frets on the A,D and G strings; make these chords ring out loud and clear.

4 Back at the 3rd and 5th frets use the first finger for the A string and ring and little fingers for the D and G strings.

TONY IOMMI

1948–
BAND: **BLACK SABBATH**
HEIGHT OF FAME: **1970s**

Tony Iommi has a good claim to be the heaviest of all heavy-rock guitarists. After all, he more or less invented heavy metal single-handedly with Black Sabbath. Sabbath's classic songs – 'Paranoid', 'War Pigs', 'Iron Man' and many others – combined brutally simple, yet monstrously effective, riffs with banshee vocals courtesy of Ozzy Osbourne and relentlessly dark lyrical imagery. With Black Sabbath, a genre was born.

RIGHT: *Tony Iommi was fundamental to heavy-rock history; indeed, some music critics have claimed that Iommi and Black Sabbath were the sole creators of the genre.*

Tony Iommi was born on 19 February 1948, in Birmingham, England, He started playing guitar as a teenager, inspired by the likes of Hank Marvin & the Shadows. By the late 1960s, Iommi had formed a group called Earth with three old school friends — bassist Terry 'Geezer' Butler, drummer Bill Ward, and singer John 'Ozzy' Osbourne. Iommi's musical career was nearly over before it began after an accident at work led to the loss of the tips of the fingers on his right hand. However, he managed to recover and adapt his style.

Iommi briefly joined Jethro Tull in 1968, but quickly rejoined Earth, now renamed Black Sabbath. They quickly developed their new direction – dark lyrical subjects backed by repetitive heavy riffs. They got the mix perfected right from the start. Their self-titled debut album was an immediate hit as were its follow-ups, 1971's *Paranoid* and *Master of Reality*, 1972's *Vol. 4*, and 1973's *Sabbath Bloody Sabbath*. By that time they were one of the world's top hard-rock bands, with Iommi's guitar playing at the heart of their sound, pumping out some of the most recognizable guitar riffs in rock history.

But by the late 1970s, constant touring and drug abuse began to fracture the band, leading to Osbourne's exit in 1979. Iommi kept the band going and it triumphantly re-formed in the late 1990s, their music acknowledged as uniquely influential.

TONY'S FINGERS

The pivotal moment in Tony Iommi's guitar-playing history was almost his last. It happened when he was 18 and the band he played in had just landed a tour of Germany. On Tony's very last day at work in a sheet-metal factory, he caught his right hand in a machine press. He instinctively pulled his hand away and as he did so, ripped off the ends of his middle and ring fingers, which were caught in the machine. Ironically enough, Iommi had actually planned on skipping work that day but his mother had insisted he go, telling him it was the right thing to do.

At first, Iommi was close to giving up on ever playing again, Then a friend gave him a record by legendary gypsy jazz guitarist Django Reinhardt, who had suffered a burn to his left hand that left him with only two working fingers. This inspired Tony to start playing again. First he experimented with playing the guitar with his other hand, but without much success. Then he came up with the rather brilliant idea of making himself thimbles for the tips of his two damaged fingers. He made them by melting down plastic bottles of Fairy Liquid (an English brand of washing-up liquid), shaping them, and then putting leather ends on them so he could grip the strings better. Then, despite not being able to feel the ends of his 'thimble' wearing fingers, Tony set about relearning how to play. Whether he would have come up with the revolutionary style he eventually arrived at without the accident we shall never know.

RIGHT: *Iommi is most identified with Black Sabbath in the late ' 60s and early ' 70s, but he has also built a successful solo career in the 2000s.*

Iron Man

ALBUM: **PARANOID**

SONGWRITERS: **TONY IOMMI, BILL WARD, GEEZER BUTLER, OZZY OSBORNE**

RECORDED: **REGENT SOUND, ISLAND STUDIOS, LONDON**

PRODUCER: **RODGER BAIN**

This is a chunky rock riff played with a two-fret gap at all times. Try to keep the notes solid and heavy; practise accuracy moving the shape around. Be careful to avoid hitting the open E bass string when bringing the plectrum down on the notes in the chord. Try to practise holding the chord shape steady, especially as you move it up and down the fret board.

BASIC SONG RIFF

HERE'S HOW

1 With the first finger at the 3rd fret of the A string and ring finger at the 5th fret of the D string hold this shape firm.

2 The riff has climbed to the 11th and 13th frets and now jumps back and forth between two frets. Keep time with the beat.

3 This is exactly the same shape back on the 8th and 10th frets of the A and D strings. Repeat the riff slowly until you feel comfortable.

TONY IOMMI'S SGs

Being left-handed, Iommi had a lot of trouble finding a guitar that suited him when he was starting out. At that time, the early 1960s, electric guitars weren't easy to get hold of at all, let alone left-handed ones.

His first guitar was a Watkins, a popular, inexpensive British copy of a Fender Stratocaster. As he moved on to a Burns (another British brand) and then to a real Strat, his choices were limited by his left-handed playing style. He did find a left-handed Strat eventually, but he preferred the sound of the Gibson SGs he'd heard, so he bit on the bullet, bought a right handed SG, and strung it upside down, just as Hendrix did with his Strat. Then, by chance, he ran into another guitarist who was right-handed but, bizarrely, happened to be playing a left-handed SG strung upside down. Tony Iommi suggested they swap, and it was this SG he played on most of the classic Black Sabbath albums. As he became successful, he was able to get custom-made left-handed guitars, all modelled on the SG shape. The best known of these are the ones made by Jaydee guitars, a company started by Iommi's sometime guitar tech John Diggins and, later on, a signature model made by British company Patrick Eggle Guitars. More recently a Tony Iommi signature model has also been manufactured by Gibson themselves – so anyone interested in reinventing heavy metal today is spoilt for choice.

RIGHT: *The Gibson SG provided Tony Iommi's ideal guitar shape, and his custom-built guitars are made to this pattern.*

Paranoid

ALBUM: **PARANOID**

SONGWRITERS: **TONY IOMMI, BILL WARD, GEEZER BUTLER, OZZY OSBORNE**

RECORDED: **REGENT SOUND, ISLAND STUDIOS, LONDON**

PRODUCER: **RODGER BAIN**

Another classic early heavy metal riff using that familiar two-fret distance between each string. You need to ensure these notes are played hard and accurately when dropping down from your E to D string. To create speed this riff also uses the hammer on technique. Use the two finger shape to create a heavy rock sound. The hammer on will increase speed and can be used to accentuate the tune.

BASIC SONG RIFF

HERE'S HOW

1 First and ring fingers are used together, the first finger playing notes on two strings at the 12th fret and the ring to hammer on.

2 Here the riff only requires you to play the A string, again use the hammer on technique but be careful to avoid hitting the E string.

3 Bring your first finger down to the D string ready to play the 12th fret, once again use the hammer on to create speed.

MICK RONSON

1946–1993

BAND: **THE SPIDERS FROM MARS, HUNTER AND RONSON**

HEIGHT OF FAME: **1970s**

Mick Ronson was the undisputed king of the glam-rock guitarists. For three tumultuous years he played a stack-heeled Keith Richards to David Bowie's preening Jagger. His riffs powered Bowie rockers like 'Jean Genie' and 'Rebel Rebel', while his melodic lead playing turned songs like 'Ziggy Stardust' into classics. What marked Ronson's style out was its mixture of simplicity and sophistication. When a straightforward catchy riff was needed, that was just what he supplied, but he was also able to supply the avant-garde sound textures which still make those 30-year-old Bowie recordings sound contemporary.

RIGHT: *Mick Ronson was a major influence on the sound of David Bowie, and played on some of Bowie's most popular tracks.*

Mick Ronson was born in Hull, Yorkshire, on 26 May 1946. He received both piano and violin lessons as a child and also played the harmonium in church before taking up guitar in his late teens. He played in various local bands, including The Rats, who would later provide the nucleus of Bowie's backing band The Spiders From Mars. But Ronson's real preparation for working with Bowie came when he added electric guitar to an album by folkie Mike Chapman, full of string-bends and unusual rhythmic sequences. Hearing this inspired Bowie, then recording the acoustic-based 'Space Oddity', to hire Ronson to add some rock edge to his material. Their combination was spectacularly successful through the early 1970s. Then, in 1974, Bowie split up the band and Ronson tried a brief solo career before teaming up with Mott The Hoople's Ian Hunter. The next decades saw Ronson working with an extraordinary variety of artists from Bob Dylan to Morrissey, via John Mellencamp and Meatloaf. He had a brief reunion with David Bowie shortly before he died of liver cancer on 30 April 1993, aged 46.

RONSON'S LES PAUL

Whenever people talk about the 1970s' guitar sound, chances are they mean something not far removed from Ronson's signature '58 Les Paul/100-Watt Marshall sound. As a member of Bowie's Spiders from Mars, Ronson gave the Les Paul an image overhaul and a thrilling new sound. It certainly didn't sound like the same Les Paul that had been played by Clapton and his fellow blues rockers. This Les Paul had an edgier, punkier sound. To get his particular sound Ronson used his Dunlop CryBaby wah as a tone shaper, working the pedal until he found the desired mid-range bite, then leaving it in that position. He was also a master at using the wah to push a solo to its squealing, wailing climax.

BELOW: *Ronson helped put the Gibson Les Paul on the map by combining it with a Dunlop CryBaby. All of Ronson's recordings in his Spiders period were made using a Marshall Major 200W amp nicknamed 'the pig'.*

The actual age and model of Ronson's much-photographed Les Paul Custom, however, remains unclear. Ronson was famously uninterested in his equipment. In a December 1976 feature in *Guitar Player* magazine, it is identified as a '58, but other articles suggest that it was actually a '68. One thing is sure: the famous Paul didn't start out with its blonde colouring.

When he was playing with Michael Chapman in 1969, Ronson admired the natural wood on the folk singer's Gibson J-200. Chapman explained that he had stripped the original finish to improve his acoustic's high-end response. Impressed, Ronson immediately directed one of Chapman's roadies to remove the black finish from his Les Paul. By the late 1970s, however, Ronson had moved on to playing Stratocasters and had sold the Les Paul to Steve Jones of The Sex Pistols – a guitarist whose sound was clearly shaped by Ronson's knack with a heavy yet poppy riff.

Rebel Rebel

ALBUM: **DIAMOND DOGS**
SONGWRITER: **DAVID BOWIE**
RECORDED: **OLYMPIC STUDIOS; ISLAND STUDIOS, LONDON**
PRODUCER: **DAVID BOWIE**

This is a lovely descending riff from David Bowie's 'Rebel Rebel'. Following the single E note intro on the D string use your ring finger to slide into the E note at the 5th fret on the B string. Practise using your first three fingers to play descending runs down the fret board. Play the riff slowly with feeling, hit the notes hard with the plectrum to get that great Mick Ronson sound.

BASIC SONG RIFF

HERE'S HOW

1 This shows the long E note on the D string – hold this note with the first finger while you find position to start the descending run.

2 Play this D note on the B string with your middle finger to allow your first finger to fall behind and hit the 2nd fret.

3 Position your first finger on the first fret of the G string and your middle finger can hit the final E note on the D string.

THE ANTI-GEAR GUITARIST

Most of the guitar greats are gear obsessives, musicians who are constantly tweaking their guitars and amps and effects to find that killer distortion sound, that perfect fretboard, or super-sensitive pickup. Others are collectors always on the lookout for that pre-war Gibson or that perfect Martin. Mick Ronson, however, was most definitely the exception to the rule.

Ronson's attitude comes over clearly in his description of playing a guest spot with David Bowie in the 1980s. He borrowed a guitar from Bowie's regular axeman, Earl Slick, and started thrashing out 'Jean Genie', whirling the guitar around his head. He couldn't understand why Slick was looking so horrified. 'Later on I found it was his special guitar. I didn't know it was his special guitar, I just though it was a guitar, a lump of wood with 6 strings.' That's certainly the attitude Ronson had to his own guitars

'I've always been the same way with guitars, they've always got something wrong with them. I'm really lazy about getting things fixed and I tend to sort of leave them. But at the same time I kind of leave them on purpose, for some psychological reason I leave them like that so I have to wrestle with them. Then it feels real to me.' And as for amplifiers, 'Often I wouldn't even think of what I was plugging into...it doesn't matter to me at all as long as it works.' Without taking Ronson's attitude to extremes, it's worth taking in the crucial fact that what really matters is what you play, not what kind of guitar you're playing it on.

LEFT: *Mick Ronson was a rock guitarist who focused all his efforts on playing, not on his equipment.*

Ziggy Stardust

ALBUM: **THE RISE AND FALL OF ZIGGY STARDUST AND THE SPIDERS FROM MARS**
SONGWRITER: **DAVID BOWIE**
RECORDED: **TRIDENT STUDIOS, LONDON**
PRODUCERS: **DAVID BOWIE, KEN SCOTT**

Here is a great example of using regular chords to create a classic riff. The intro to 'Ziggy Stardust' is based around the G and D chords with a few extra notes to make it more interesting. Listen to how Mick Ronson plays around the D chord during the intro. You can use the chords in this song to experiment using single chords as a melodic intro to a tune.

BASIC SONG RIFF

HERE'S HOW

1. The middle finger holds down the bass note G on the E string, the ring and little fingers play notes on the B and E strings.

2. D chord – you can either play this with your middle, ring and little finger or first finger across three strings with your little finger on the D note.

3. Your middle finger should play the C note on the A string and your third finger plays the D note on the B string.

4. Your first finger plays the B note on the A string; release your middle finger and play the D note on the B string.

DAVID GILMOUR

1946–
BAND: **PINK FLOYD**
HEIGHT OF FAME: **1970s–80s**

Some guitarists become legends thanks to their phenomenal technique, others because of their originality. Then there are those whose reputation rests heavily of the uniqueness of their tone. Names like Stevie Ray Vaughan, Eric Clapton and B.B. King might be mentioned in this context, Carlos Santana certainly, but perhaps the ultimate tone guitarist is Pink Floyd's David Gilmour. The sound of Gilmour's blues-influenced, but not exactly bluesy, Stratocaster playing on *Dark Side Of the Moon* has come to define progressive-rock guitar playing.

RIGHT: *Pink Floyd was an experimental group in nature, and David Gilmour was its ideal guitarist, someone with a superb playing skill combined with an interest in effects.*

David Gilmour was born on 6 March 1946 in Cambridge, England. He began playing acoustic guitar at age 14, before moving on to Burns Sonnet and Hofner Club 60 electrics. While still at school, Gilmour met Roger Waters and Syd Barrett. Waters and Barrett put together Pink Floyd in 1965 along with keyboardist Rick Wright and drummer Nick Mason. When Barrett's drug use began to make him unstable Gilmour was drafted into the group first as back-up and then as a replacement for Barrett.

Over the next few years the band became ever more experimental, making albums like *Ummagumma* and *Atom Heart Mother*. At first Gilmour was playing a Telecaster but, after it was stolen, he replaced it with a Strat, played through HiWatt amps, and soon a variety of effects pedals. The band took most of 1972 off to work on a new studio album. This was *Dark Side Of The Moon* and overnight it established Pink Floyd as a major league rock act. The album stayed on the charts longer than any other record in history. Follow-ups *Wish You Were Here*, *Animals*, and *The Wall* all sold in their millions and the Pink Floyd sound, with Gilmour's spacey guitar at the fore, has continued to appeal to successive generations of rock fans.

HOW TO GILMOUR-IZE YOUR STRAT

Gilmour's main stage guitar is a USA '57 Vintage Reissue Strat fitted with a shortened tremolo arm so that he can keep it in his picking hand more comfortably while playing. The other modifications are all on the electrical side.

Like all his Strats, it's loaded with low impedance EMG-SA single coil pickups, which he backs up with two more tone modules, an SPC mid booster and an EXG mid-cut/expander. The SA pickups have Alnico magnets which have a little more mid range than the ceramic S magnets. The SPC midrange boost control is used to produce more of a singing humbucker tone, while the EXG is used a great deal for rhythm, since it really helps define the notes, especially when distortion is being used. The EXG cuts the mid range right down while giving a hefty boost to both the bass and treble.

It's with the use of the SPC, though, that you really hear the Gilmour sound emerge. Turn the SPC all the way up and you get that thick bluesy sound with which he is always associated. Then there's the tremolo arm, an important part of Gilmour's sound but notoriously prone to send the guitar out of tune. Gilmour tries to minimize this by screwing down the front six screws on top of the tremolo faceplate as far as possible in order to make total contact. He feels this keeps the bar in better tune.

RIGHT: *The Fender Stratocaster has been one of the seminal instruments of the rock and pop era. It was designed by Leo Fender in 1953, and is still in production, in its modern form, today.*

Wish You Were Here

ALBUM: **WISH YOU WERE HERE**
SONGWRITERS: **DAVID GILMOUR, ROGER WATERS**
RECORDED: **ABBEY ROAD STUDIOS, LONDON**
PRODUCERS: **PINK FLOYD**

These are the acoustic guitar chords to 'Wish You Were Here'. The song starts with two acoustic guitars moving around these chords – the first plays the chords and the second guitar picks out a melody. Experiment with removing and adding a finger to these chords to vary the sound. Once you've mastered these chords, singing along will help you get the timing of the rhythm right.

BASIC SONG RIFF

Em^7

G

A^7sus^4

$G*$

HERE'S HOW

1 This shows the first finger on the E note at the 2nd fret of the D string. The ring and little fingers should play the B and E strings.

2 This is simply the chord shape shown previously with the first finger removed, keep the ring and little fingers in position.

3 The ring and little fingers stay at the 3rd fret of the B and E strings; the first finger and middle finger play the D and G strings.

4 The first finger plays the A string, the middle plays the E, the ring and little fingers still on the B and E strings at the 3rd fret.

THE CORNISH BOARD

Gilmour's first Cornish board consisted of a two guitar input selector and strobe tuner feed, while the actual effects were a Dallas Arbiter Fuzz Face, an MXR Phase 100, Dynacomp and noise gate, a Uni-Vibe, Pete Cornish Custom Fuzz, and a Jim Dunlop Cry Baby. The board featured three Cry Baby sweep pedals. These were modified as tone control, volume pedal and wah-wah respectively. This new state-of-the-art board had sophisticated switching capabilities that were far ahead of most late 1970s' pedal set-ups. Each effect could be individually bypassed or configured in any sequence, and there were three outputs for various amps. This may not sound so extraordinary in today's all digital, post-Midi environment but back then, using analogue technology, it was revolutionary.

Despite the apparent complexity of Dave Gilmour's set-up, the actual contents of each track may come as something of a surprise. Essentially his sound is fairly clean, choosing different distortion units to add their characteristic sound to his signal. As an example, to reproduce the track 'Money' from *Dark Side Of The Moon* live in concert, Gilmour uses this effects combination. Main Riff: Pete Cornish Soft Sustain with Chandler Tube Driver #2. Solo: Boss CS-2 Compressor with Chandler Tube Driver #1, Sovtek Big Muff & TC Electronics digital delay. Solo (Dry Sound): Chandler Tube Driver #1 with Pro Co. Rat II Distortion.

Pete Cornish now has his own business making custom effects and boards, so, if you think your playing needs a sophisticated effects set-up that's easy to manage on stage, you'll be in good company if you look him up.

LEFT: *The bewildering array of effects pedals available to David Gilmour during live performances.*

Money

ALBUM: **DARK SIDE OF THE MOON**
SONGWRITERS: **ROGER WATERS**
RECORDED: **ABBEY ROAD STUDIOS, LONDON**
PRODUCERS: **PINK FLOYD**

This song has a great walking bass-note line. The tab shows the opening notes of the song which sounds really good played on an electric guitar with no effects. It takes a little practice but once it's in your head it's a joy to play. Keep the notes thick and distinct. Keep in mind the recorded version – thinking of the sound of the cash registers crashing should keep you in time!

BASIC SONG RIFF

HERE'S HOW

1 Here the first finger plays the A string at the 2nd fret. Get your ring finger ready to play the 4th fret of the G string.

2 The ring finger plays the 4th fret of the G string. You can also play this phrase with your ring finger on the D string and little finger on the G.

3 You'll need your little finger to stretch to the 5th fret. Keep your other fingers in position to repeat the phrase from the start.

MULTI-EFFECT USE

In the early days of rock, guitarists tended to confine themselves to using one or two effects – generally either fuzz or wah-wah in full-on fashion. Gradually, though, as these effects became better known, and more types of effects came on to the market, guitarists started to experiment with sound, pioneering ever more complex combinations of effects. David Gilmour was in the forefront of this trend.

At the time of *Dark Side Of The Moon* he was using, amongst other things, a wah-wah, an Electro-Harmonix Big Muff, a Uni-Vibe and a Maestro Rover. The problem with using several effects at once, however, was that if they were wired up in series there tended to be a significant fall-off in the quality of the sound. Plus the simple fact of having half a dozen battery-operated pedals on stage meant there were any number of things that could go wrong. Then Gilmour heard of a man called Pete Cornish who worked for Sound City in London. Cornish had started making custom effects units, black boxes operated by foot switches, inside which Cornish would wire all the necessary electrics for each of the desired effects units. Gilmour got in touch with Cornish and began a working relationship that has gone on for more than 20 years.

RIGHT: *Gilmour has been noted for his use of the whammy bar, using it to create a mournful, song-like tone on some of Floyd's most famous tracks.*

Time

ALBUM: **DARK SIDE OF THE MOON**
SONGWRITERS: **DAVID GILMOUR, ROGER WATERS, NICK MASON, RICK WRIGHT**
RECORDED: **ABBEY ROAD STUDIOS, LONDON**
PRODUCERS: **PINK FLOYD**

This tab shows the part of the riff after all the alarm clocks go off. It's basically two notes on the E string with long gaps before the main part of the songs kicks in. It's obviously a fairly easy riff to play but you need to get the timing spot on. To get the best effect it's best to play this riff along with the record, and this will also help with your timing.

BASIC SONG RIFF

HERE'S HOW

1 This shows the first finger on the F# note at the 2nd fret of the E string. Hit this note nice and hard after skipping up from the open E string via the first fret.

2 This picture shows the little finger at the A note on the 5th fret of the E string. Keep your first finger at the F# note.

LEARN TO PLAY LIKE THE GUITAR GREATS

BRIAN MAY

1947–
BAND: **QUEEN**
HEIGHT OF FAME: **1970s–90s**

Queen's Brian May has one of the most instantly recognizable guitar sounds there is.

It's a huge, almost orchestral, sound, perfectly suited to his band's own unique fusion of

pop and rock.

Brian May was born in a suburb of London, England in July 1947. He was a musical child, able to play the ukulele and piano by the time he was given his first guitar on his seventh birthday. The instrument immediately fascinated May and, while still at school, he went on to build – with his father's help – an electric guitar. Amazingly enough this instrument, known as the Red Special, and costing just £8 to make, has been the principal guitar he has played throughout his career.

May's career started with a school band called 1984. He then went on to play with the rather more successful Smile, which provided the nucleus for Queen. Queen's first album came out in 1973, and by the time of lead singer Freddie Mercury's death in 1991 they had established themselves as one of the most globally popular bands of all time. The band's twin strengths were Mercury's showmanship and May's knack for an instantly memorable riff – whether the one that comes in midway through 'Bohemian Rhapsody', or the one that underpins 'We Will Rock You'. Equally distinctive was May's deeply melodic lead work. May has released several solo albums, hosted the Guitar Legends concert alongside Steve Vai and Joe Satriani, and overseen the enormously successful Queen-tribute stage musical *We Will Rock You*. In 2005 Queen returned to touring with former Free and Bad Company vocalist Paul Rodgers on guest vocals.

RIGHT: *Brian May has created some of the most memorable guitar riffs in history. With Queen, and writing for other artists, he has composed 22 top-20 hits.*

THE RED SPECIAL

Not many guitarists have kept one main guitar with them throughout their entire career. Surely it is only May who has managed that feat using a guitar he made himself when still at school.

The guitar was made up mostly of materials May found lying around: mahogany from a fire surround for the neck of the guitar, a piece of oak for the centre block, motorbike valve springs for the tremolo springs and mother-of-pearl buttons for the neck position dots. A particularly interesting innovation was to have the three pickups wired in series, rather than in parallel as is conventional. Each pickup has an on-off switch and a phase change switch. The combination allows a huge variety of different sounds. Initially the pickups too were homemade, but May didn't care for the sound and eventually replaced them with Burns Tri-sonic single coils.

The Red Special may be a one-off, but aspiring Brian Mays will be relieved to learn they won't have to build their own copies. Ever since Queen's rise to fame there have been an abundance of imitations on the market. May himself has used an assortment of them as back-up live guitars. Copies have ranged from the frankly dodgy to the absolutely exquisite. Top of the range are the Guyton Red Special Guitars handmade by Andrew Guyton, with a price tag to match their quality; ordinary mortals might want to investigate the more workaday, but very dependable, Burns Brian May Signature Electric Guitar.

RIGHT: *Brian May's Red Special is as legendary as the guitarist himself. May created the guitar from scratch, and he has always possessed a deep understanding of the technical aspects of music production and instrumentation.*

We Will Rock You

ALBUM: **NEWS OF THE WORLD**
SONGWRITER: **BRIAN MAY**
RECORDED: **SARM WEST; WESSEX STUDIOS, LONDON**
PRODUCER: **MIKE STONE**

This is the first guitar entry into 'We Will Rock You'. Make sure you get that nice big power chord sound like Brian May on the first chord. In this riff you'll also use your ring finger to hit that low G note on the E string. Practise using your ring finger to hit that bass note on the E string, as this will give the riff an extra punch.

BASIC SONG RIFF

HERE'S HOW

1 This shows the first finger at the 3rd fret of the A string and the ring and little fingers at the 5th fret of the D and G strings.

2 Try using your first finger here to cover both strings at the same time at the 2nd fret on the D and G strings.

3 This is the bass note at the 3rd fret of the E string; play this with your middle finger, and try a little bend on this note.

PLAY LIKE BRIAN

So how do you get that signature Brian May guitar sound? Well first you need the right equipment. Ideally, of course you should have a decent Red Special replica, a Burns or Guild maybe. Failing that, a Les Paul will get you somewhere close. Next there's the amp. May favours using several classic 1960s Vox AC 30s all turned up to the max to produce the required overdrive, but don't try this at home unless you live several miles from the nearest neighbour. For domestic use, many classic amps – a Marshall or a Mesa Boogie say – will do a decent job with the gain kept down and the mid range EQ turned up. What you will definitely need, though, is a treble booster pedal. If you want to get every last detail right you could even use an old British sixpence coin as a guitar pick, just like Brian does.

That's the simple part, however. What is not so easy to copy is the actual playing. Having said that, Brian May's guitar parts are far from the most difficult in the business; Queen's pop/rock focus never encouraged pyrotechnics for their own sake. May's rhythm work is mostly based on using open chords with that distinctive ringing overdrive produced by the AC 30s. His soloing, meanwhile, utilizes his preferred light-gauge strings to allow a lot of string-bending and vibrato plus plenty of hammer-ons and pull-offs. The key to his style is always to focus on keeping things melodic, while giving the music a hard, strong edge.

LEFT: *In Queen, Freddie Mercury was undeniably the frontman, but May was the driving force behind the music itself.*

Bohemian Rhapsody

ALBUM: A **NIGHT AT THE OPERA**
SONGWRITER: **FREDDIE MERCURY**
RECORDED: **ROCKFIELD STUDIOS, WALES**
PRODUCER: **ROY THOMAS BAKER**

This is the guitar riff just before Freddie Mercury sings 'so you think you can stone me and spit in my eye'. Although only played over two strings it does move around a fair bit and will require some practice to perfect. Use up and down strokes with your plectrum to get extra speed. Try to make the notes distinct – it's a riff where every note counts. Experiment with different ways of playing until you feel comfortable.

BASIC SONG RIFF

HERE'S HOW

1 You need to give yourself as much stretch as possible between the first two notes on the E and A strings – use your first and little finger here.

2 Here the middle finger plays the G note at the 3rd fret of the E string. Take your time to get it right.

3 The little finger plays the 8th fret on the A string. Note the basic shape of the fretting hand is the same throughout.

Tie Your Mother Down

ALBUM: **A DAY AT THE RACES**
SONGWRITER: **BRIAN MAY**
RECORDED: **SARM WEST; WESSEX STUDIOS, LONDON**
PRODUCER: **MIKE STONE**

For this famous Queen riff use your first finger to cover both second frets on the D and G strings at the start of the riff. You will need to keep your ring finger to hit notes on the E and A strings. Play along with the track to ensure your timing is spot on. Use down strokes with the plectrum to create a heavy rock sound. Practise down strokes between the high and low strings on the guitar.

BASIC SONG RIFF

HERE'S HOW

1 The hand is ideally positioned to play all notes shown in the tab. The ring finger can move easily to the A and E strings.

2 Here the ring finger moves up to the A string to play the C note at the 3rd fret. The first finger stays in position.

3 By using your first finger for notes at the 2nd fret you are leaving your middle, ring and little fingers available for notes on the top strings.

FAR LEFT: *Brian May's career has now spanned three decades. Versions of his songs have been recorded by artistes as diverse as Def Leppard, George Michael and Macy Gray.*

NILE RODGERS

1952–
BAND: **CHIC**
HEIGHT OF FAME: **1970s**

Nile Rodgers is the godfather of funk guitar. Ask anyone for their definition of funky rhythm-guitar playing, and they'll like as not refer you to Nile Rodgers' playing on Chic's 'Le Freak' or 'Good Times'. His sinuous, choppy rhythm parts – brilliantly combined with the equally distinctive bass playing of Bernard Edwards and drumming of Tony Thompson – have come to define funk.

RIGHT: *Nile Rodgers performing at a live gig. He first joined a band when he was 16, telling the other members he could play guitar when he couldn' t. He was a fast learner, however, and his natural talent soon emerged.*

Nile Rodgers was born on 19 September 1952 in New York City. He came from a musical family and his talent was evident from his early years. By the time Nile was 19, he was playing guitar as part of the house band for the world famous Apollo Theatre, accompanying a whole range of soul legends. He met Bernard Edwards in the early 1970s. At first they put together a series of rock bands, but the music industry wasn't interested in a group of black guys playing rock music. So they turned their attention to dance music and formed Chic. From their first hit, 'Dance Dance Dance (Yowsah Yowsah Yowsah)', through to 'Le Freak' and 'Good Times', their sound defined the disco era.

At first critics tended to dismiss them as commercial pap, but when musicians started to listen carefully they realized this was one of the tightest units in any kind of music. Rodgers' guitar playing in particular influenced everyone from Queen's Brian May to Prince, and his reputation spread even wider as he turned his hand to freelance writing and producing. Suddenly his unmistakably funky sound could be heard on records by acts as diverse as David Bowie, Madonna and Diana Ross. His influence, meanwhile, is still present every time a rock guitarist decides it's time to get funky and tries to imitate those deceptively simple rhythm patterns.

FUNK GUITAR

Nile Rodgers may be the best known proponent of funk guitar playing – and he certainly developed a style that is uniquely his own – but he'd be the first to acknowledge that his playing comes out of a tradition. If there's one man who actually did invent funk guitar playing, it's Jimmy Nolen. His name may be unfamiliar, but as the guitarist on practically all James Brown's classic recordings his playing most certainly isn't. Nolen developed his pervasive funk style during his 16 years with Brown. Although he was primarily a rhythm guitarist, the impact Nolen had on subsequent players was no less important or far reaching than the influence of rock and blues innovators like Chuck Berry, or B.B. King. His distinctive style of 16th-note strumming and funky, choppy chord work (relying heavily on 7th and 9th chords) provided the foundation on which virtually all modern R&B, funk and disco guitar is based.

Nile Rodgers' style has its roots in Nolen's playing and also encompasses the influence of jazz guitarists like Wes Montgomery – it's noticeable that Rodgers uses a lot of jazz chords in his playing. The other defining funk guitar sound is the use of the wah-wah pedal in rhythm playing, as typified by the theme from *Shaft*. Rodgers uses this effect from time to time, while offering the following valuable advice to would-be proponents of the style. 'Never keep time with the pedal,' he cautions. 'Use it for expression, and keep time with your hands.'

LEFT: *Nile Rodgers has emphasized the need for a good sense of rhythm to be a competent funk guitarist, and has avoided an over-reliance upon electronic gadgets.*

Le Freak

ALBUM: **C'EST CHIC**
SONGWRITERS: **NILE RODGERS, BERNARD EDWARDS**
RECORDED: **THE POWER STATION, NEW YORK**
PRODUCERS: **NILE RODGERS, BERNARD EDWARDS**

This great dance tune uses up and down strokes to create that classic Nile Rodgers clicking rhythm. The best way to achieve this is to use your thumb instead of a plectrum. Take time to practise playing rhythmically up and down whilst moving the chord between the 7th and 5th frets. The dampening technique will cut off the sound. You can do this by slightly releasing the hand holding the chord after it's played.

BASIC SONG RIFF

HERE'S HOW

1. Shows the start of the riff as the band sing 'Ah....' Use your first finger to cover both 5th frets on the E and B strings.

2. Practise this part in isolation. Hammer-on with your ring finger onto the 7th fret whilst your first finger holds the 5th frets.

3. You can use your ring finger across three frets at the 7th, then release leaving your ring finger to cover the 5th. Practise that rhythm with your thumb.

PRINCE

1958–
BAND: **PRINCE AND THE REVOLUTION**
HEIGHT OF FAME: **1980s**

Prince is one of the most versatile of all modern guitar players and also, as a result, one of the most underrated. He can play in classic rock style, all screaming arpeggios played high up on the neck. Live, if the mood takes him, he can play like Jimi Hendrix, the full sonic freak out. Then again, if he chooses, he can play classic 1970s funk style, using the wah-wah pedal on the rhythm fills. Keep in mind that he's also an extraordinary singer-songwriter and showman, one of the real auteurs in popular music, and it's unsurprising that his guitar playing sometimes gets overlooked.

Prince was born Prince Rogers Nelson on 7 June 1958 in Minneapolis, Minnesota. His father gave him his first guitar. Prince quickly showed a prodigious musical talent on a whole range of instruments and as a singer-songwriter, and signed a major deal with Warner Bros while in his teens. His first album, *For You*, released in 1978, saw him playing all the instruments himself. On subsequent albums he moved from the fairly straight soul of his debut to more rock- and even punk-influenced material. At this point his Hendrix-inspired guitar playing came to the fore.

His career picked up momentum and he achieved a huge breakthrough with *Purple Rain*, an album that saw him melding rock and funk influences. The album would sell over 13 million copies in the US alone, and spend 24 weeks at the top of the Billboard 200. It established Prince as a superstar. Backed by a succession of phenomenal bands, Prince seemed able to channel almost every style of rock and soul that had gone before – and every style of guitar playing too.

RIGHT: *Prince delivered some of the most electrifying live performances of the 1980s and 1990s, astounding audiences as much with his dancing as with his obvious musicality.*

PRINCE'S TELECASTER COPY

It's easy to assume that all great guitarists use top-of-the-range equipment that costs a fortune. It may be true that, as they get richer, guitar players tend to accumulate more and more expensive guitars, but it's also true that some of them have made much of their best work using less exalted instruments.

Prince is a case in point. Almost all the records that made his reputation feature a Hohner Telecaster copy. Given that many guitarists disdain the Telecaster itself in favour of the Stratocaster, to use a Telecaster copy seems the height of cheek. The guitar in question was bought in 1980 from the Knut Koupee Music store in Minneapolis. According to the store's manager, Prince probably chose the guitar because of its leopard-skin pickguard, which matched his stage outfit! But as it turned out, the budget guitar's raw tone was ideal for the clean guitar chugging and staccato rhythms of his early Punk-Funk style. He used it whilst supporting Rick James that year, on the *Dirty Mind* album, and on almost every tour to date.

A Telecaster variant, the guitar differs greatly to the Fender industry standard. The Hohner is all maple and finished in blonde, as opposed to the ash and alder body of a Fender. The tonal properties of maple suit Prince well, giving the guitar a bright top end and good sustain; he chose this wood for all his later custom guitars. The cheaper construction of the guitar gave rise to problems in the studio, but Prince still insisted on using it, favouring its tone which he once described as 'raggedy'. Discontinued re-issues of the guitar can still be tracked down.

LEFT: *Prince is one of that rare breed of successful guitarists who have stuck with a cheaper model of instrument on account of what they feel is a rawness of sound.*

Purple Rain

ALBUM: **PURPLE RAIN**

SONGWRITER: **PRINCE**

RECORDED: **SUNSET SOUND STUDIO, LOS ANGELES**

PRODUCER: **PRINCE**

These chords sound absolutely great with nothing else at the start of 'Purple Rain'. To get the sound exactly the same as Prince you'll need to use a chorus pedal on an electric guitar. Practise getting the timing right just before the vocal comes in at the start of the first verse. Ensure your chords flow naturally from one another, and practise moving between these shapes to get a really smooth sound.

BASIC SONG CHORDS

C

Am7

G

F

Fsus4

HERE'S HOW

1 This is a C chord. Use your first, middle and ring finger to hold these notes. Use single down strokes with your strumming hand.

2 By releasing your ring finger you'll form the next chord in the sequence which is Am7. Keep your rhythm regular as you change between each chord.

3 Use your first finger to play the B and E strings, your ring finger to play the D string, and your little finger for the G string.

SLASH

1965–
BAND: **GUNS N' ROSES**
HEIGHT OF FAME: **LATE 1980s**

The man behind some of the most enduringly popular guitar riffs of the past 20 years, Slash was born in London, England, in 1965 to parents who both worked in the music business. In the 1970s he relocated to his mother's home town of Los Angeles. He began playing guitar in high school and soon formed the most popular American rock band of the late 1980s, Guns N' Roses, along with singer Axl Rose, co-guitarist Izzy Stradlin, plus high-school buddy Steven Adler on drums and Duff McKagan on bass.

RIGHT: *Slash gave Guns N' Roses their hard rock edge. He lists amongst his influences Jimmy Page, Mick Taylor, Eddy Van Halen and Jeff Beck.*

Their first album, *Appetite For Destruction,* came out in 1987 and still stands as one of the all-time classic hard-rock recordings. It took a year to catch on, but once MTV started playing the video for the album's power ballad 'Sweet Child O' Mine', success was assured. *Appetite For Destruction*, full of snarling twin-guitar workouts like 'Welcome To The Jungle' and 'Paradise City', revived the outlaw spirit of The Rolling Stones and Aerosmith. It went on to sell over 30 million copies. The band never quite scaled such heights again, though follow-up *Use Your Illusion* came close. As the 1990s wore on the band suffered from musical differences and drug problems, and from the mid 1990s onwards, Slash has pursued a solo career.

As a guitarist Slash's style owes most to his early heroes The Rolling Stones and, above all, to Aerosmith's Joe Perry. Over time, a blues feel has come into his playing, and Slash now cites Jeff Beck – blues-based but always experimental – as his biggest inspiration. Meanwhile, guitar shops around the world have signs forbidding novices from emulating Slash's killer guitar part 'Sweet Child O' Mine', recently voted the finest guitar riff of all time by readers of *Total Guitar* magazine.

NO ORDINARY RIFF

'Sweet Child O' Mine' is something of an odd one out among the classic guitar riffs. For a start it powers a ballad rather than an up-tempo number. Second, instead of being made up of power chords played low down on the guitar, it uses arpeggiated chords played very high on the neck. Thirdly, where most of the great riffs are blissfully straightforward and direct, 'Sweet Child O' Mine' is positively tricksy. Maybe that's why every would-be guitar hero feels compelled to learn it: it's become something of a rite of passage.

What it does have in common with many rock classics is that it was a bit of a musical afterthought. The band already had the songs for their classic debut album when they started jamming on some chords Izzy Stradlin had come up with. Axl Rose started singing the words from a poem he'd written some time before. Meanwhile, Slash was messing round with a little guitar pattern high up on the neck. The rest, of course, is history. Without 'Sweet Child O' Mine', Guns N' Roses might never have got off the ground. It's a great Zen lesson for all guitar heroes – sometimes it's when you're not really thinking that you're actually doing your best work.

SLASH & THE GIBSON LES PAUL

One of the all-time classic rock guitars, the Gibson Les Paul had fallen somewhat out of fashion by the late 1980s before Slash brought it right back in.

He'd first played a Memphis Les Paul Copy while in school, nailing Ted Nugent's 'Cat Scratch Fever' with it. Later, he bought a real Les Paul that had once belonged to ex Alice Cooper/ Lou Reed guitar legend Steve Hunter. When the *Appetite For Destruction* sessions started, Slash was playing a Jackson. He was unhappy with the sound and increasingly desperate when his manager found him what appeared to be a '59 Les Paul. In fact it was a handmade copy made by luthier Chris Derrig. Slash fell in love with it and promptly used the new guitar to write the riff to 'Sweet Child O' Mine'.

Since then, the guitar has become his signature instrument for both live and studio work. Today, it has been retired, due to the stresses of live work, but Slash's love affair with the Les Paul has continued. Indeed the company has issued not one but two limited-edition custom Slash Les Pauls, the first a loud and proud fire burst with mother of pearl inlay and hand painted Snakepit logo, the second a rather more austere tobacco burst instrument.

ABOVE: *Slash's handling of the Gibson Les Paul is all the more remarkable when understanding that he is almost entirely self taught, learning mainly through imitating great riffs from records.*

Live and Let Die

ALBUM: **USE YOUR ILLUSION I**
SONGWRITERS: **PAUL MCCARTNEY, LINDA MCCARTNEY**
RECORDED: **A & M STUDIOS; RECORD PLANT; STUDIO 56; IMAGE RECORDING, HOLLYWOOD**
PRODUCERS: **MIKE CLINK, GUNS N' ROSES**

This is the part of the song where the orchestral string section plays the same riff as the band. If you want to play along with the record you'll need to tune your guitar down a semitone. The riff is played on this tab on the top three strings (E, B and G). Practise getting a distinct sound from each note in the riff. Keep in time by playing with the record.

BASIC SONG RIFF

HERE'S HOW

1 Use your first, middle and ring fingers to climb up the frets on the E string. Practising this will help you play lead runs more easily.

2 This is the same riff on the B string. Try to move easily between the two. Imagining the sound of the orchestra will help keep you in time.

3 These descending notes are played with the ring and first finger on the G string. The last note is B flat – hold it and let it ring out.

KURT COBAIN

1967–1993
BAND: **NIRVANA**
HEIGHT OF FAME: **1990s**

Just as Kurt Cobain was the epitome of the anti-pop star, an idol who hated to be idolized, he was also the ultimate anti-guitar hero, a riff master who took pleasure in playing out of key on bargain-basement instruments. As with his band Nirvana as a whole, his strength wasn't in subtlety or technique, but in raw passion and the most brutal of dynamics.

RIGHT: *Kurt Cobain's raw playing was the defining quality of grunge and a direct reaction against the musical dexterity shown by many guitarists in the world of heavy rock.*

If Cobain's contribution to guitar playing can be narrowed down, it's his perfection of the quiet/loud contrast. He didn't invent it – The Pixies were doing something similar years before – but Cobain took the business of alternating between quiet and loud to its ultimate, brain-shredding extreme.

Kurt Donald Cobain was born to Wendy and Donald Cobain on 20 February 1967 in Aberdeen, Washington State. His mother was a cocktail waitress and his father an auto mechanic. In high school he started listening to punk rock and on his fourteenth birthday he bought his first guitar. He dropped out of high school a few weeks before graduation to get a job, and started playing in bands. In 1986 he formed Nirvana with Krist Novoselic on bass guitar, and, eventually, Dave Grohl on drums. Their first album, *Bleach*, was released in 1989 and was only a minor hit, but they toured incessantly and signed to Geffen Records, who released their second album, *Nevermind*, which included the classic guitar riff of the 1990s, 'Smells Like Teen Spirit', alongside songs like 'Lithium' which showcased their quiet/loud dynamic. As they achieved success however, Cobain's life plunged into drug abuse and self-loathing. He married Courtney Love, recorded a new album, *In Utero*, but was evidently hell-bent on self-destruction and, in 1993, one week after a concert in Munich, was hospitalized in a coma. After waking up and leaving voluntarily, he was found three days later in his own home, dead of a gunshot wound.

KURT'S FENDERS

Kurt Cobain generally played either Fender Mustangs or Fender Jaguars, left-handed models. These are unusual choices for a top guitarist, being fairly cheap guitars without the build quality of the Stratocaster or even the Telecaster.

Kurt Cobain initially started playing them for reasons of economy – especially relevant given his penchant for destroying guitars on stage (at one time he was calculated to have destroyed over 300 guitars). However, perverse character that he was, it was also their defects that attracted Cobain to these models. Of the Fender Mustang he once commented that 'My favourite guitar in the world is the Fender Mustang. They're really small and almost impossible to keep in tune. They're designed terribly. If you want to raise the action, you have to de-tune all the strings, pull the bridge out, turn these little screws under the bridge, and hope that you've raised them the right amount. Then you put the bridge back and tune all the strings. If you screwed up, you have to do the whole process over again. But I like it, that way things sound fucked-up, and I stumble onto stuff accidentally. I guess I don't like to be that familiar with my guitar.' A more unusual approach to the guitar is hard to imagine.

Throughout his career Cobain found it hard to decide between the Mustang and its sister guitar, the Jaguar. The guitar he played on most of *Nevermind* was a 1965 sunburst (red faded out) Fender Jaguar. Eventually, unable to chose between the two, and now famous and rich enough to have what he wanted, he persuaded Fender to create a custom guitar for him, the Jag-Tang – a mutant beast that, as its name suggests, was half Jaguar and half Mustang.

BELOW: *Kurt Cobain's use of fairly cheap Fender guitars was reflected in a playing style, which often featured sloppy technique (by orthodox standards) and questionable tuning, but always a great sound.*

Smells Like Teen Spirit

ALBUM: **NEVERMIND**
SONGWRITERS: **KURT COBAIN, KRIS NOVOSELIC, DAVE GROHL**
RECORDED: **SOUND CITY, LOS ANGELES**
PRODUCER: **BUTCH VIG**

A fantastic intro to a classic Nirvana song. It's all power chords on the bass strings so you need to ensure you hold the shapes firm as you move them around the fret board. It's best to listen to the record to get the rhythm exactly right with your strumming hand. The first part of the riff is played clean with no overdrive, then the distorted guitar comes in to really drive the riff along.

BASIC SONG RIFF

HERE'S HOW

1 Here the first finger plays the first fret on the E string with the ring and little finger playing the A and D strings at the 3rd fret.

2 The shape of the chord drops down one string, the first finger plays the 1st fret of the A string, the ring finger can play all three frets of the D, G and B strings.

3 The first finger plays the 4th fret of the E string, the ring and little fingers play 6th fret of the A and D strings.

4 For the last chord, the shape again drops down one string, with the first finger playing the 4th fret of the A string and the ring finger playing the 6th fret on the D, G and B strings.

JACK WHITE

1975–
BAND: **THE WHITE STRIPES**
HEIGHT OF FAME: **EARLY 2000s**

Jack White is a man on a mission – taking rock 'n' roll back to basics. As the mainstay of The White Stripes he's emerged as a formidable songwriter, guitarist and vocalist capable of morphing between styles from folk blues through show tunes to full-on Led Zeppelin-style rock workouts. The band's third album, 2001's *White Blood Cells*, established the duo at the forefront of the new wave of rock 'n' roll bands. They also managed the remarkable feat of appealing to both MTV kids and their parents with their mix of the sophisticated and the primitive, adding up to an instinctively classic style.

RIGHT: *In The White Stripes Jack White has stripped rock music down to its absolute basics – distorted guitar and a thumping drum beat in the background.*

Jack White was born John Anthony Gillis on 9 July 1975, in Detroit, and played in assorted punk and garage bands before forming The White Stripes with his then wife Meg (using the rumour that they were brother and sister as a sales gimmick). His back to basics style is evident both in his playing, which nods to everyone from the Kinks' Dave Davies to Led Zeppelin's Jimmy Page, and in his choice of equipment. At the heart of White's sound is his main guitar – a '64 Valco Airline. On stage, White carries three guitars: the Airline, a Kay hollow body tuned to open A, and a no-name Japanese electric. He plugs into a DigiTech Whammy pedal and an Electro-Harmonix Big Muff, before running simultaneously into a Fender Twin Reverb and a rare 100-Watt Silvertone 6x10 combo.

Some find this fondness for vintage equipment, which extends also to their studio work, self-consciously retro. But whatever your preference – analogue or digital – it is undeniable that Jack White understands the primitive power of rock 'n' roll. One listen to a classic riff like 'Seven Nation Army' should convince anyone of that.

VALCO AIRLINE GUITAR

Just as punk rock rebelled against established music industry values, so punk guitarists rebelled against conventional guitar lore. Not for them the Les Pauls and Stratocasters, let alone the Paul Reed Smiths and high-end custom jobs.

The über-punk guitarist, Johnny Ramone, favoured 1960s Mosrites; Kurt Cobain went for the ugly sisters of the Fender range, the Mustang and Jaguar; and Jack White went a step further by playing a JB Hutto model 1964 Valco Airline, a guitar that most players might regard as good for having your picture taken with, but wouldn't be caught dead actually playing. It's made of fibreglass (or 'Res-O-Glas' as the manufacturers called it), which makes it difficult to keep in tune; there's no way of adjusting the pickup or the action. It's a cheap guitar, and that's something Jack White is well aware of. As he says himself 'Playing that guitar makes me feel like I have to take something that's broken and make it work. It's hollow, it's made of plastic, and it feels like it's going to fall apart. The front pickup is broken, but the treble pickup has an amazing bite. I've never had it refretted or anything. It's pretty much the way I found it, except for new tuners."

Now increasingly sought after by wannabe Jack Whites, Airline Guitars were made by the Chicago-based Valco factory, an offshoot of National-Dobro, and mostly sold by mail order giants Montgomery Ward. Their other popular model was the Silvertone and, during the 1960s, Valco produced both guitars by the truckload. These days, the guitars turn up regularly on Ebay, no longer the pawn shop bargains they were before Jack White came along.

RIGHT: *The Valco Airline has won little praise for build quality or technical sophistication, but its distinctive sound has made it the choice of guitarists such as Jack White. Vintage examples can sell for several thousand dollars.*

Seven Nation Army

ALBUM: **ELEPHANT**
SONGWRITER: **JACK WHITE**
RECORDED: **TOE RAG STUDIOS, LONDON**
PRODUCER: **JACK WHITE**

These are terrific power chords that require you to turn up your amp and play loud! Once again note the two-fret interval; ensure you hit the lowest note first for maximum effect. Get used to moving the shape around the fret board. Start off slowly and build up speed. The tab shows the riff in baritone tuning, but you can play in standard tuning using the A, D and G strings.

BASIC SONG RIFF

HERE'S HOW

1   Use your first finger at the 7th fret and ring and little fingers to play the 9th fret. Practise keeping these chords solid.

2   Hit the first chord twice then slide straight up to this position at the 10th and 12th frets. Concentrate on keeping your shape.

3   Let this last chord ring out, your fingers will keep the same shape throughout. Use only big down strokes with your plectrum.

BLUES GUITARISTS

Today, when we think of the blues we immediately think of the guitar. It was not always so, however. Back in the 1920s, when the first records with the word 'blues' in the title were being made, more often than not they'd be piano-led recordings, close in style to the jazz and gospel recordings of the same period. If you listen, for instance, to the recordings of the enduring icon of 1920s blues, Bessie Smith, you'll be searching in vain for a guitar part; instead you'll hear sophisticated piano and brass arrangements, played by the likes of Fletcher Henderson and Coleman Hawkins, or even Benny Goodman.

BELOW: *T-Bone Walker is one of the legends of blues guitar, and was a person who developed an early love affair with the instrument in his teens.*

The origins of blues guitar are really bound up with just one style of blues – one that had relatively little commercial impact at the time but was to prove enormously influential ever since – and that's country blues, in particular the Mississippi Delta Blues. Delta Blues began to emerge around the turn of the century on the cotton plantations that lined the Mississippi. These plantations were often the size of small towns, and the black labourers who worked the fields could spend their whole lives in such a place, in conditions barely changed since the abolition of slavery little more than a generation before.

One of these plantations, Dockery's, was home to a young man named Charley Patton, who was to become the father of Delta Blues. He wasn't the inventor of the style; its roots, in fact, can be traced all the way back to West African musicians singing and playing a guitar-like instrument called the kora. Patton himself learned to play and sing from older musicians who lived on the plantation, including one Henry Sloan. However, Patton was the first to be recorded and to pursue a career playing the music in public.

What really marked out Charlie Patton's style – and that of all the early Delta blues men – was that the guitar was no longer used as simple accompaniment, designed to underpin a vocal melody just as a piano does. Instead it provided a fierce counterpoint, even an extension, of the human voice. The singer calls out a line and the guitar answers back.

BLUES PIONEERS

Charlie Patton was to prove a huge influence on subsequent guitarists. His immediate protégé was the great Son House, responsible for records like 'Death Letter'. Son House, in turn, was to prove a great influence on a young musician named Robert Johnson, who, in part thanks to the legends that surround him, has become the one country bluesman that even casual listeners have heard of.

Robert Johnson introduced the boogie bass line, played on the bottom strings of the guitar, which now practically defines what we think of as 'blues guitar'. His slide playing was the most developed yet heard, and he added a repertoire of rundowns and turnbacks and repeats that almost defied belief – and have taken the world's finest guitar players decades to figure out. No wonder rumour had it that Johnson had sold his soul to the devil one night at the crossroads near Dockery's plantation.

The Mississippi Delta wasn't the only place to produce country blues musicians, however. Notable contemporaries of Charlie Patton included this formidable trio – all of them, by some strange coincidence, unsighted. There was Blind Lemon Jefferson from Texas, Blind Willie McTell from Georgia and Blind Blake from Jacksonville, Florida. Blind Blake had a prodigious ragtime-derived guitar style which musicians to this day have trouble deconstructing. While he was popular in his day, he disappeared without trace in the early 1930s, so he was never rediscovered and subjected to the scrutiny of blues scholars. Blind Willie MacTell was another formidable guitar

ABOVE: *Robert Johnson led a short, tough life in the early decades of the 20th century, but his superb blues playing was later to influence the likes of Eric Clapton and Keith Richards.*

ABOVE: *Gibson guitars have been a popular choice amongst the world's greatest blues guitarists, B.B. King being one of their most high profile users.*

talent who combined use of slide and fingerpicking on classic songs like 'Statesboro Blues' to make it sound as if he was playing two guitars at once.

Blind Lemon Jefferson was, in his day, the most influential of all. He was the first man to be a truly commercially successful blues performer. Unlike the blues women such as Bessie Smith who had ruled the roost before him, he didn't have a band but performed solo, accompanying himself on the guitar on genre-defining songs like 'Matchbox Blues', 'See That My Grave Is Kept Clean' and 'Black Snake Moan'.

Texas has remained a blues stronghold ever since, with artists ranging from T-Bone Walker to Albert King to Stevie Ray Vaughan. However, it was the Mississippi Delta bluesmen who were to be the dominant influence on what was to come. Gradually, in the years following Robert Johnson's death, the blues made its way north, up the river to Memphis, and then to Chicago, and along the way it became electrified. In fact the first major electric blues player was the Texan T-Bone Walker, whose jazz-inflected Gibson playing sent out shockwaves through the blues world. However, it was in the hands of Delta-born talents like B.B. King and Muddy Waters that electric blues guitar developed to the next stage.

B.B. King is almost certainly the single most important electric blues guitarist of the last half century. His style, full of vibrato and melodic invention, has been so influential that it is hard to conceive of a contemporary blues guitar solo that doesn't feature at least a couple of recognizable King-derived phrases.

If B.B. King represented an increasing sophistication in blues playing, his contemporary John Lee Hooker kept alive its anarchic primitive roots. Hooker's signature tracks, like 'Boogie Chillen', are one-chord boogies in which the guitar is turned all the way up and used to project rhythm and menace.

If there's a mid point between King and Hooker it would probably sound like Muddy Waters. Muddy Waters started out playing country blues down in the Delta, but when he came to Chicago he defined the city's aggressive, swaggering, Delta-rooted sound with his utterly confident vocals and ferocious slide-guitar attack. Technical excellence has never sounded so menacing.

Or at least not until contemporaries of Muddy's, like Bo Diddley and Howlin' Wolf guitarist Hubert Sumlin, started to kick in. Sumlin was a stunningly inventive player both on lead and rhythm duties behind the primeval roar of the Wolf, while Bo Diddley managed to cross Muddy's dynamics with John Lee Hooker's rolling one-chord boogie and African rhythms to create a sound so irresistibly catchy that it even managed to cross over to the white rock 'n' roll audience.

Up to this point in its history, the evolution of blues guitar playing – and the blues itself – had been straightforward. It was music that had originated with rural Southern blacks as an acoustic folk form, and had evolved into the electric music of urban blacks. Now, though, it was about to take a most unexpected turn.

Across the Atlantic, in the UK, a generation of young white kids had picked up on the blues and were starting to attempt to play it themselves. At first their efforts were pale imitations, but gradually some of these young Brits began to seriously come to grips with the form, and also to add in elements of their own. In the lead was a young Londoner called Eric Clapton, whose style owed plenty to both B.B. King and his fiery Texan namesake Freddie King. Whether or not Clapton was actually as skilled or as original a blues musician as his heroes is open to debate. What is certain, however, is that he became the very first 'guitar hero' and opened up a huge new white audience for the blues. Thanks to his popularity Chicago bluesmen like Muddy Waters and Buddy Guy, whose careers had been tailing off with the rise of soul music within the black communities, enjoyed new lease of life.

In America too, white bluesmen started to come to the fore. Chicago produced Michael Bloomfield, who contributed blistering guitar work to Bob Dylan's early electric period. That other great blues centre, Texas, produced first the albino Johnny Winter, a fiery player whose finest hour might just be the records he cut with Muddy Waters in the late 1970s, and then Stevie Ray Vaughan. Vaughan is arguably the most influential of all the white bluesmen – not merely a follower, he was also an innovator, and it's rare to hear a young blues guitarist today, whether black or white, who doesn't owe something to the ultimately full-on style of SRV.

HISTORY OF THE SLIDE GUITAR

There are many theories as to the origin of the slide guitar. W.C. Handy famously recalled hearing an unknown musician using a knife on the strings of his guitar. But this unknown

BELOW: *Albert King's visual trademark was his Flying V guitar, an instrument that few other contemporary musicians adopted.*

bluesman had scarcely invented the style. For centuries musicians around the world have created sounds by dragging objects across stringed instruments. One example is the West African musical bow. This is a one-stringed instrument attached to a gourd resonator, and held against the body, while the player plucks the string and uses a bone or metal to vary the pitch.

This was probably the ancestor of a bowed instrument called the Jitterbug used by African-American musicians around the Southern states of America at the turn of the century. The Jitterbug, like the bow, had one string, but this time it was attached to the floor instead of a gourd. When plucked, an object would be dragged along the string to accompany simple songs. This produced a wailing/moaning sound well suited to the early blues. The scraping technique was no doubt adapted to the guitar, once cheap models started to be available from mail-order catalogues even in the many rural backwaters.

Meanwhile a different kind of slide guitar, a forerunner of what we now know as the lap steel, was being pioneered in Hawaii. This became enormously popular after a young Hawaiian guitarist called Joseph Kekeku made some popular recordings using the steel guitar around the turn of the century. It was a flashy, eerie kind of sound that became very popular, and the Hawaiian-style lap steel started to outsell Spanish-style guitars. Soon the use of the slide began to seep into all styles of music, from the early blues to the mountain music of the Appalachians. Whatever the origins of the slide guitar, however, it is certain that it reached its apotheosis in its partnership with the blues.

TWELVE-BAR BLUES

The 12-bar blues progression is the main underpinning of the vast majority of blues tunes out there. So, in order to start playing, you'll need to know

BELOW: *Stevie Ray Vaughan had a talent comparable to the great Jimi Hendrix, but his life was cut short by a helicopter crash in 1990.*

what a 12-bar blues progression is. The basic concept of the 12-bar blues is the I-IV-V progression, where I, IV and V represent the chords that you will be using.

When you play a basic blues progression, you will only need to use three chords. The principle of I-IV-V tells you which chords to use. It's essentially a slightly oversimplified approach to figuring out which chord to use next. It's based on a numeric system, linked to the letters of the alphabet. Say you're playing in C, then the C chord will be the I; you then count three letters further up the alphabet to get to F, which will be the IV chord. Count one further letter forward and you get to the G chord and that will be the V. It's not an infallible system but it works for the keys of A, C, D, E and G, which will keep you going for a while. Thus, for the key of A, we will be using A-D-E as our I-IV-V progression. Likewise if you count out starting with E, you will find that for the key of E we will use E-A-B as our I-IV-V. Music theory terminology, by the way, calls the I the 'tonic', the IV the 'subdominant', and the V the 'dominant'.

So how to put the chord progression into use? The basic concept of the 12-bar blues is to create and resolve tension. Once you get used to the progression, you will see how the V generally creates tension in your progression and the I generally resolves tension. It may be useful to think of the 12-bar progression as divided into three mini-sections of four bars each.

Here's a simple 12-bar progression: I-I-I-I-IV-IV-I-I-V-IV-I-I/V. The first four bars (I-I-I-I) just sort of set things up, using the relaxed I chord. In the second four-bar segment (IV-IV-I-I) a little tension is introduced by switching to the IV chord for bars five–six, but resolved by switching back to the I chord in bars seven–eight. Then in the third four-bar segment (V-IV-I-I/V) the tension is increased in the ninth bar, when we switch to the V chord for the first time. The tension is gradually resolved in bars 10–11 before using a two chord 'turnaround' to set up the next 12 bars.

BELOW: *Eric Clapton, here seen in his younger days, has been one of the formative figures in modern guitar playing, not least in bringing the blues into mainstream music.*

ROBERT JOHNSON

1911–1938
BAND: **SOLO ARTIST**
HEIGHT OF FAME: **1930s**

Robert Johnson is where it all starts. His country blues style is the cornerstone of modern blues. His guitar playing still remains the gold standard as far as acolytes like Eric Clapton and Keith Richards are concerned. When his few recordings were gathered together for a double CD in 1990 they went on to sell over a million copies, helped by the legends that surround the man.

RIGHT: *Robert Johnson lived only a short life, dying at the age of 27 after having been deliberately poisoned. He did, however, leave his mark on the world of guitar playing.*

From what little we know of him, Johnson had a short life and a violent death. Chief among the many legends that surround him is the story that he acquired his extraordinary ability on the guitar thanks to a pact he made with the Devil himself, after meeting him one dark night at a Mississippi crossroads.

While it's a great story, the truth is more prosaic. Johnson actually practised. He learnt a lot from his first idol, the Delta recording star Lonnie Johnson – as well as from Skip James and Kokomo Arnold. He developed his slide style after much listening to fellow Delta bluesmen Charley Patton and Son House. The big leap forward his guitar playing took in the mid 1930s followed a year or so learning from an unrecorded bluesman named Ike Zinneman, a man who liked to practise late at night in the local graveyard. Following this tuition, Johnson seemed to have complete mastery of his instrument, and an ability to sing and play in whatever style was needed in order to make a living as an itinerant musician.

It was with his blues numbers, however, that his individuality shone through. He introduced the boogie bass line played on the bottom strings of the guitar, which now practically defines blues guitar. Add to that a repertoire of rundowns and turnbacks and repeats and Johnson had taken the guitar to the next stage.

ROBERT JOHNSON'S THUMB BASS STYLE

Back in the early 1960s, so the story goes, just when The Rolling Stones were starting out, Keith Richards played Mick Jagger a Robert Johnson record. Jagger listened to it and asked who the bass player was. Keith laughed and told him there wasn't one.

What Johnson was doing was playing a kind of bass line using his thumb on the bottom three strings of the guitar, while playing the melody on the top two strings, all at the same time. It's a style that has become basic to what we think of as blues guitar today. The bass figure, played with the thumb, provides the rolling boogie. It's not a new musical idea, it's the same basic principle as the piano player using his or her left hand to provide the bass. It's just a little trickier to enact on a guitar, because the same hand has to play both parts simultaneously, something which is every bit as hard as it sounds.

Robert Johnson of course was blessed with unusually large hands and long fingers, which were a help, but essentially to master this technique you're going to have to practise very hard indeed. Once mastered, though, it's a wonderfully adaptable technique, and you don't even need to vary it all that much, Robert Johnson used very similar thumb bass patterns in almost half his recorded songs, including the likes of 'Love in Vain', 'Me and the Devil', '32-20 Blues', 'Stop Breakin' Down', 'Steady Rollin' Man' and 'Honeymoon'.

LEFT: *Robert Johnson's large hands and long fingers are evident in this photograph.*

Crossroad Blues

ALBUM: **COMPLETE RECORDINGS**
SONGWRITER: **ROBERT JOHNSON**
RECORDED: **GANTER HOTEL, TEXAS**
PRODUCER: **N/A**

This is a great blues lick starting at the top end of the guitar neck. Try to get that Robert Johnson lonesome ringing sound when you play the first few notes of 'Crossroad Blues', listen to the way it rings out high before eventually dropping down a semitone. Keep your notes clean to achieve that ringing sound. Use down strokes to get that incessant rhythm during the opening.

BASIC SONG RIFF

swing

HERE'S HOW

1 This shows the first and ring fingers holding the shape on the F# and D# notes on the E and B strings.

2 Release the ring finger so that the middle finger can play the D note on the B string; this creates that descending sound.

3 The riff has moved up to the G and D strings. Use your first and little fingers for these notes to allow yourself maximum stretch between each note.

SLIDE GUITAR

Robert Johnson is one of the first names most people think of when it comes to playing acoustic blues slide guitar. However, it wasn't Johnson who invented it. In fact, as far back as 1903 W.C. Handy – the man who liked to call himself 'the father of the blues' – told a story about falling asleep on a bench in a railway station in the Mississippi Delta town of Tutwiler while waiting for a train. He was awakened by the sound of a man singing and playing guitar in unorthodox fashion – rather than fretting the neck with his fingers, he was sliding a knife up and down the strings.

This was evidently slide-guitar playing in its earliest form. Essentially, slide guitar is the technique of using a smooth, hard object – usually a hollow metal or glass cylinder, for instance a bottleneck, rather than a knife – to change the pitches of the strings. The origins of the style have been traced back to African one-stringed instruments and also to Hawaiian guitar styles. Early bluesmen who used slide guitar techniques included Eddie 'Son' House, Tampa Red before Robert Johnson, and the likes of Muddy Waters and Elmore James after him. What it offers guitar players is a whole variety of effects – glissandos, voice-like cries – and also access to the notes between the frets. Therefore it's an invaluable style for anyone interested in playing acoustic blues guitar. There are plenty of commercially available slides on offer, or if you want to be traditional you can use anything from a bottle neck to a lipstick holder. Then tune your guitar to open D and start practising.

LEFT: *A blues guitar player is here seen using a professional slide, although in the history of the great blues guitarists everything from bottles to knives have been used.*

Me and the Devil

ALBUM: **COMPLETE RECORDINGS**
SONGWRITER: **ROBERT JOHNSON**
RECORDED: **GANTER HOTEL, TEXAS**
PRODUCER: **N/A**

The tab shows a descending chord shape that stays the same as it drops from the 8th and 9th frets to the 6th and 7th frets. Experiment with similar shapes on other parts of the neck to get unusual note combinations and ringing sounds heard in lots of blues songs. Keep your strumming regular as you move down the frets. Practise accuracy when moving these shapes around the neck.

BASIC SONG RIFF

swing

HERE'S HOW

1 Use your first finger to play the 8th fret on the B string, your middle finger on the G string and your ring finger plays the E string.

2 We have now dropped a whole tone. When you've hit this chord your ring finger will be released from the fret board to anticipate the next position.

3 Use your first finger to play the E and B strings and the 5th fret and your middle finger to play the 6th fret on the G string.

T-BONE WALKER

1910–1975
BAND: **SOLO ARTIST**
HEIGHT OF FAME: **1940s**

T-Bone Walker was the blues' first true lead guitarist, and undeniably one of its very best.

Modern electric blues guitar can be traced directly back to this Texas-born pioneer, who first

plugged into an amp around 1940 and completely changed the face of music in the process.

All the great blues guitarists who came after owe him a debt.

Aaron Thibeault Walker was born on 28 May 1910 in Linden, Texas. His stepfather, Marco Washington, played the bass with the Dallas String Band, and T-Bone soon learned the basics of every stringed instrument he could. One musician the band played with regularly was the legendary Blind Lemon Jefferson, and the young Walker started to assist the great bluesman as he played around the Texas bars.

Walker made his own recording debut in 1929 with a single 78 for Columbia. In 1933 he played with another guitarist named Charlie Christian who would later electrify jazz in the same way as Walker electrified the blues. Soon afterwards Walker moved to Los Angeles and played in big bands for a living, while developing a fascination with the new electric guitar in club gigs, where he would also develop an acrobatic stage act, featuring stunts like playing the guitar behind his back or with his teeth.

Walker's guitar playing on record was notably fluent and melodic. He signed to Capitol Records and had a string of hits including the immortal 'Call It Stormy Monday' in 1947. Other hits included 'T-Bone Jumps Again', which showed he could do up tempo as well as mellow, 'T-Bone Shuffle' and 'West Side Baby'.

Walker carried on recording right up till his death in 1975 but today, it is the controlled power of his work in the 1940s and early 1950s that marks him out as one of the all-time blues greats.

RIGHT: *T-Bone Walker's first musical instrument was a banjo, bought for him by his mother when he was 12. However, he longed to play the guitar so saved up his money from playing at church social events and bought his first guitar in his early teens.*

GIBSON ES 250

The guitar T-Bone Walker is generally associated with is the Gibson ES 250, an impressive hollow-bodied instrument with a wonderfully mellow tone, and only the second electric guitar ever made by Gibson.

The ES-250 first appeared in the 1940 Gibson AA catalog with the slogan: 'Gibson has created the best electric guitar possible to make.' This top-of-the-line instrument was an upgraded version of the popular ES 150. It had significant refinements which distinguished it from the earlier mid-range model. These included a larger body, a more deluxe fingerboard, headstock, tuners and tailpiece, and a bar pick-up with individual mini-blades acting as separate pole pieces for each string for 'maximum tonal reproduction'. The ES 250, complete with case, cord and the matching EH 185 amplifier, cost the enormous sum of $250 on its launch in 1940. This meant its use was for the most part confined to the successful working professional – in short, musicians like T-Bone Walker. Charlie Christian, the great jazz player, was another early adopter – unsurprisingly as he had already made his name playing Gibson's previous model the ES 150. Other notable users included 1940s big-band guitar players such as Alvino Rey and Tony Mottola.

The high price of the ES 250s meant that a relatively small number of them were ever produced and models are now very scarce indeed. A pristine example, complete with its original case and matching Gibson EH 185 amplifier, was recently sold for no less than $27,500, which makes $250 not such a bad investment after all!

BELOW: *T-Bone used his Gibson guitars to bring traditional acoustic blues riffs to the electric guitar.*

Stormy Monday Blues

ALBUM: **BORN TO BE NO GOOD; STORMY MONDAY (LIVE)**
SONGWRITER: **T-BONE WALKER**
RECORDED: **BLACK & WHITE RECORDS**
PRODUCER: **N/A**

This is a great slow blues tune by T-Bone Walker, and sounds best on an electric or semi-acoustic guitar. These are nice chords to play around with, adapt and add to your repertoire. The fingering takes a bit of getting used to, so practise moving around these shapes. This tune sounds best played slowly and mournfully.

BASIC SONG RIFF

HERE'S HOW

1 The first finger covers notes at the 3rd frets of the G and B strings, middle finger on the D, ring plays 5th fret of the A string.

2 First finger on the 3rd fret A string, middle finger on the G string, ring finger on the D string and little finger plays the B string.

3 Here the first finger plays the 3rd fret of the D string and your middle finger covers the three frets of the G, B and E strings.

B.B. KING

1925–
BAND: **SOLO ARTIST**
HEIGHT OF FAME: **1950s–PRESENT**

For more than half a century, B.B. King has defined the blues for a worldwide audience. Since he started recording in the 1940s, he has released over 50 albums. A fine blues singer, he is also one of the most influential guitar players of all time. His particular contributions are his utterly distinctive use of vibrato and the use of space in his guitar solos. Where later guitarists are all about warp-fast blurs of notes, King specializes in playing a few well-chosen notes, and enhancing them with different techniques (such as vibrato and string bending) to create something remarkably close to the human voice. If there a guitarist who can truly make his instrument sing, then it is surely B.B. King.

He was born Riley King on 16 September 1925, on a plantation in Itta Bene, Mississippi, near Indianola. He started out playing on street corners for dimes. In 1947, he hitchhiked to Memphis, where he stayed with his cousin Bukka White, already a top blues singer. After a while he landed a gig hosting a blues radio show, and was given the B.B. (Blues Boy) nickname.

It wasn't long before King had a number one R&B hit of his own, 'Three O'Clock Blues'. He then began touring nationally, and in 1956 played an astonishing 342 one-night stands. He's kept at it ever since, playing everywhere from the juke joints and dance halls of his early days to new concert halls and amphitheatres. Along the way, he has become the most renowned blues musician of the past 40 years, and one of the most identifiable guitar stylists.

RIGHT: *B.B. King has been one of the hardest-working blues performers in history. His love of live performance has kept him on the stage even throughout his seventies.*

LUCILLE

BELOW: *One of B.B. King's Gibson Lucille guitars on display at 'B.B. King's Nightclub' in Universal City, California.*

In the mid 1950s, while King was performing at a dance in Twist, Arkansas, a fight broke out between some men in the audience, which led to the hall catching on fire. The story goes that King ran back in to the burning hall to save his guitar, risking death in the process, Afterwards, having discovered that the fight had been over a woman named Lucille, he decided to give the name to his guitar. Ever since that time, he has named each one of his trademark Gibson guitars Lucille.

The current Lucille is a Gibson ES 355. B.B. has been playing this model for at least 25 years. Prior to that time, he played an ES 335. The main difference between the two guitars is that the ES 355 is a solid body. B.B. likes to think of the ES 355 as the 'big brother' of Gibson's Les Paul.

Although King has a special relationship with Gibson guitars, he has played plenty of other guitars along the way. His very first guitar was a Stella acoustic and early in his career, he played and owned many different makes, such as Fender, Gretsch and Silverstone.

In his publicity, King emphasizes the notion that the guitar is a woman. He called a 1968 album Lucille and wrote in the sleeve notes that 'I'm very crazy about Lucille. She's taken me a long way, even brought me some fame ... most of all, she's kept me alive, being able to eat ... Lucille practically saved my life two or three times. Sometimes I get to a place I can't even say nothing ... sometimes when I'm blue, seems Lucille tries to help me, calls my name ... She's just like a woman, and that's the only one I've had that seemed I could really depend on. I've been married and each time separated from my wife, but Lucille never separates from me. She always stayed with me.'

Sweet Sixteen

ALBUM: **VARIOUS COMPILATIONS**
SONGWRITER: **B.B. KING, JOE BIHARI**
RECORDED: **VARIOUS RECORDINGS**
PRODUCER: **N/A**

This is an unmistakable B.B. King intro all played at the top end of the fret board. Bending strings from one note to another creates a lovely lonesome and bluesy feel. Try to get used to playing at the top end of the fret board. Always check your tuning after practising bending notes. Build up strength in your middle and ring fingers to make bending easy.

BASIC SONG RIFF

HERE'S HOW

1. You can use a hammer-on technique to play the first two notes in this intro at the 14th and 16th frets of the G string.

2. Dropping to the B string, your middle finger can play the 15th fret of the B string to allow your ring finger space to play the lovely bend.

3. By using middle and ring fingers to play the notes and bends high up the fret board you can leave your first finger to play the lower notes.

GIBSON LAB SERIES L5

B.B King generally plays Lucille through a Gibson Lab Series amp. What's unusual about that is that the L5 is a solid-state amp rather than a tube amp. Most pro guitar players turn their noses up at solid-state amps, seeing them as cheap in terms of both price and tone quality. Not sure about the difference? Put simply, tube amps have a number of tubes that contain a lot of scientific stuff like plates, grids and cathodes which end up moving energy around, resulting in sound reproduction. A solid-state amp only features integrated circuits and transistors.

Historically, tube amps are more expensive, based on the increased number and nature of the components. Tube amps may also be affected by climate, so consistency and reliability in the tubes are important. Tube amps are much heavier than solid-state amps, due to the additional output transformer. So why do so many guitarists like them?

Essentially it is the warm tone of tube amps that draws guitarists to them. On the other hand, they offer a less consistent tone that solid-state amps, and this may well be one of the factors that drew B.B. King to the Lab Series amps.

The Gibson Lab Series L5 combo guitar amplifier was a 100-Watt, 2-channel (non-switching) 2 - 12" speaker combo that was in production from roughly the late 1970s to the early 1980s. It has four inputs, a rather unusual built-in compressor, reverb, and a 'mid-frequency' knob that controls the mid range of the amplifier. It also has speaker outputs, pre-amp inputs, etc., but no effects loop. Although the amp is branded a Gibson, it was actually manufactured by a company called Norlin for Gibson.

RIGHT: *A young B.B. King is here seen practising with one of his 'Lucilles'.*

The Three O'Clock Blues

ALBUM: **VARIOUS COMPILATIONS**
SONGWRITERS: **B.B. KING, JULES BIHARI**
RECORDED: **VARIOUS RECORDINGS**
PRODUCER: **N/A**

This is a lead lick played mainly on the top strings. It also takes you high up the neck, so mastering this riff will enable you to move up and down the fret board with ease, which will help develop essential skills for good lead-guitar playing. Practise bending notes through a whole tone on high strings; to do this you' ll need to bend notes two frets higher.

BASIC SONG RIFF

HERE'S HOW

1 The intro notes are played on the B string with the first and ring finger. Make sure you play these notes hard and with clarity.

2 You now need to take this D flat note and bend it two frets up to an E flat, all on the E string.

3 This shows the little finger playing the E string at the 17th fret whilst the 1st finger is back and ready to play the 14th fret.

FOLLOWING THE VOICE

When he was asked about the almost vocal quality of his guitar playing, B.B. King commented that, 'When I sing, I play in my mind; the minute I stop singing orally, I start to sing by playing Lucille.' It's a valuable lesson to learn that guitar playing can resemble singing – for just as a singer phrases words to invest a lyric with emotion, adding particular stresses and rhythmic content, so the guitarist can phrase runs of notes in an expressive, unique way.

King is a master at using vibrato to emphasize just the right note in such a way that the phrase jumps out at the listener. He understands that if a guitarist truly wants to communicate emotion he or she does not necessarily have to play a huge number of notes in quick succession; soulfulness, not manual dexterity, is what the listener wants. What B.B. King teaches us is that, in playing blues guitar, economy and phrasing are all important. It's something he has learned through the experience of being a singer as well as a guitarist; a singer's phrasing comes just as naturally to his guitar work as it does to his voice.

King's playing is also influenced by previous generations of blues guitarists like Blind Lemon Jefferson and T-Bone Walker. When it comes to his own playing, he used precise and complex string bends played with left-hand vibrato, to give the guitar an almost vocal tone. His phrasing always respects and enhances the sentiment of the song, producing guitar work that's as emotionally compelling – whether mournful and bluesy, or joyful and rocking – as it is technically satisfying.

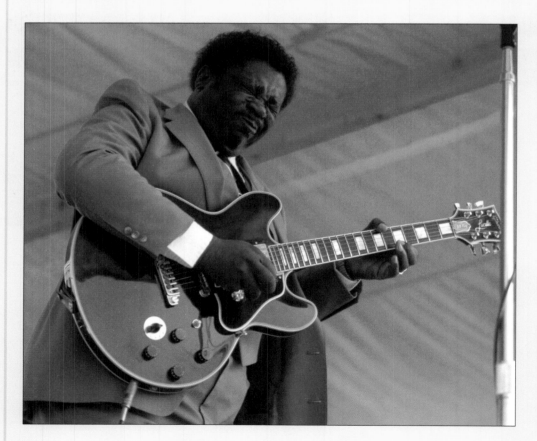

LEFT: *B.B. King has expressed a certain distance from the 'purists' of the blues community, but he has done more than almost any other artist to bring blues into the mainstream.*

Sweet Little Angel

ALBUM: **VARIOUS COMPILATIONS**
SONGWRITERS: **B.B. KING, JULES BIHARI**
RECORDED: **VARIOUS RECORDINGS**
PRODUCER: **N/A**

This great B.B. King blues tune is very melodic and starts up high on the A string. It's a good tune to practise moving between your first and ring finger over a three-fret gap. It's a great riff to experiment with and adapt to your playing style. Keep it slow, steady and smokey ! Learn to move up and down fluently between the strings at the top end of the guitar neck.

BASIC SONG RIFF

HERE'S HOW

1 Keep your first finger in position over the 8th fret on the D string whilst letting your little finger play this note at the 11th fret on the A string.

2 This is a one fret hammer-on between the 9th and 10th frets on the G string; use your first and middle fingers here.

3 Play this note at the B octave with your little finger. It sounds great if you slide into it after the notes on the G string.

ALBERT KING

1923–1992
BAND: **SOLO ARTIST**
HEIGHT OF FAME: **1960s–70s**

One of the three great blues Kings – along with B.B. and Freddie – Albert King is one of the major influences on blues and rock guitarists from Otis Rush and Robert Cray to Eric Clapton and Stevie Ray Vaughan. Yet, though his imitators have been many, few have come close to replicating Albert's own extraordinary tone.

Partly this is because he played guitar left-handed, but rather than play a left-handed guitar, or even re-stringing a right-handed guitar as Jimi Hendrix did, he simply played the guitar upside down so the bass strings are at the bottom rather than the top. As a result he pulls down on the same strings that most players push up on, thus producing a unique sound.

Albert King was born on 25 April 1923, in Indianola, MS. He taught himself to play guitar as a child, building his own instrument from a cigar box. At first, he played gospel music, but after hearing delta blues men like Lonnie Johnson and Blind Lemon Jefferson, he turned to 'the devil's music'.

He settled in St Louis in the mid 1950s. There he started playing his signature Gibson Flying V guitar and became a top local attraction, scoring his first national R&B hit. His big breakthrough came in 1967 when he signed to Stax records and released a string of singles backed by Booker T and the MGs. The combination was irresistible on numbers like 'Born Under A Bad Sign' and 'Cross Cut Saw', and the sound was an immediate hit both with the R&B audience and the new young white rock audience. Suddenly, at the age of 43, Albert King was a star, performing to packed-out audiences at the Fillmore in San Francisco and elsewhere. His recording career tailed off in the late 1970s, but as an inveterate showman he remained a major live draw until his death in 1992.

RIGHT: *Albert King has been described as the 'master of the single-string attack', and he had the ability to create perfect, clear blues phrases in the mould of Blind Lemon Jefferson and Elmore James.*

FLYING V

Back in the mid 1950s Gibson Guitars president Ted McCarty decided that his company's image needed updating. Rock 'n' roll had revolutionized the popular music scene and flamboyant characters like Bo Diddley had started playing their own customized guitars. McCarty, a trained engineer, decided to respond to this challenge by designing commercially produced guitars that completely dispensed with the old rounded acoustic-style shape of most electric guitars. In 1958, Gibson unveiled three radical new models: the Flying V, the Explorer and the Moderne.

The industry was shocked and uncertain. The Moderne never made it into commercial production while the Explorer and Flying V – so called for its revolutionary v-shape – were produced only in very limited quantities. Those guitar shops that did order them generally used them as novelty display items rather than promoting them as playable instruments. Albert King was one of the few brave souls actually attracted by the radical-looking Flying V, but too few others followed suit. Less than a hundred Flying V guitars were sold, and Gibson moved on to other new models, shelving the Flying V for a decade. It was only revived in the 1960s as the musical climate became more experimental, and again in the 1970s when the Flying V suddenly became the guitar of choice for heavy-rock groups like Wishbone Ash and The Scorpions. Original Flying Vs now have a considerable rarity value, selling for tens of thousands of dollars. Subsequent Flying Vs have had significantly different specifications to the originals, but in the 1990s Gibson manufactured a small number of custom copies of the 1958 originals. However, these have a list price of over $13,000, so hardly constitute a viable way for most guitarists to reproduce the exact sound of Albert King.

BELOW: *The Flying V guitar had little commercial success, Albert King being one of its few high-profile patrons.*

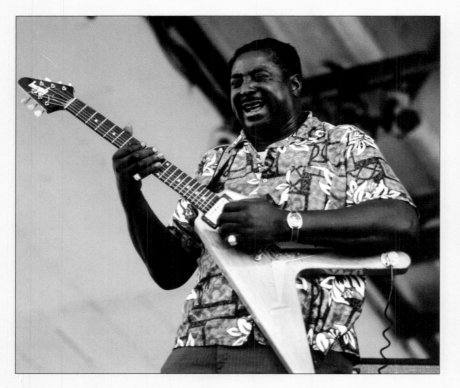

A typical Albert King lead lick

Here's the start of the kind of lead lick that Albert King incorporated into many of his blues tunes. It's played around the top B and E strings and features four climbing notes before sliding up to a screeching A note at the 10th fret of the B string.

Try to change the speed during the riff – speed up when you ascend the scale, then slow down to play that mournful slide up at the end.

BASIC RIFF

HERE'S HOW

1 Use your index finger to start the run at the 5th fret of the B string. Use your little finger to play the next note at the 8th fret of the B string.

2 Next bring your index finger up to the 5th fret on the top E, again using your little finger to play the 8th fret, this time on the top E.

3 Now use your little finger to slide from the 8th fret of the B string up to that A note at the 10th fret of the B string.

ERIC CLAPTON

1945–
BANDS: **YARDBIRDS, JOHN MAYALL'S BLUESBREAKERS, CREAM, DEREK AND THE DOMINOES**
HEIGHT OF FAME: **1970s–PRESENT**

Eric Clapton was the original guitar hero. Before Clapton, the guitarist was seen as just another musician in the band, standing behind the singer. A few aficionados might know who was hot, but the general public had no idea. Then came Clapton. His playing, first with the Yardbirds and then with John Mayall's Bluesbreakers was so startling, so incendiary, that an amazed audience started to spray paint the slogan 'Clapton is God' around London. Not that Clapton himself was too impressed by this. He was an unwilling hero, a quiet man who just wanted to get on with making music.

Clapton was born in Surrey in southern England in 1945. He started playing the blues while at art school in the early 1960s and acquired a Kay guitar. Soon afterwards he joined the Yardbirds, then left (to be replaced by Jeff Beck) when he decided they were becoming too commercial. His brief stay with John Mayall's Bluesbreakers was pivotal. In this band he was allowed to give his blues playing free rein.

Clapton's guitar hero period peaked with his next band, Cream, a hard-rock trio in which he could solo for as long as he liked. After the band split up he made one classic album with Derek And The Dominoes, featuring his masterpiece 'Layla', before succumbing to heroin addiction for several years. Once recovered, his comeback record, *461 Ocean Boulevard*, saw him playing acoustic guitar and dobro much of the time, the mood downbeat and song-based. Through the 1970s and 1980s his work headed into commercial pop-rock, before coming back to basics in the 1990s with a series of traditional blues albums.

RIGHT: *Eric Clapton, pictured here at a 1988 concert in New York, has done more than almost any other artist to bring blues into the mainstream, although he is equally known for his talents in rock and pop.*

CLAPTON'S ELECTRIC GUITARS

Clapton has had two major loves as far as electric guitars go. Through his early years, up till the demise of Cream, he was a Gibson Les Paul man. Since then – and following the influence of Jimi Hendrix who persuaded so many British guitarists to make the same switch – it's been Fender Stratocasters all the way (most famously the cannibalized instrument known as 'Blackie' which he auctioned for $450,000 for his Crossroads charity).

ABOVE: *Clapton's 'Blackie' guitar became one of rock's most expensive instruments.*

The signature instrument of Clapton's early guitar hero days was a rather more flamboyant instrument. The guitar started life as a 1961 Les Paul SG. In advance of the band's first US tour in 1967 he asked the Dutch artist collective, 'The Fool' (responsible for several other pop-art projects, mostly for The Beatles), to give the instrument a custom psychedelic paint job. The result was an impressively psychedelic instrument entirely in keeping with the times. Times change though, and following the break-up of Cream Clapton switched guitars and gave the Fool Guitar to a singer songwriter called Jackie Lomax who was making a record for Apple. Two years later a new American guitar hero about town, Todd Rundgren, happened to meet up with Lomax and was horrified to find the Fool Guitar in beat-up condition. He gave the hard-up Lomax $50 and had the guitar restored to its former glory, using it both on stage and in the studio until the guitar became too fragile to risk doing further damage.

BLACKIE

During the early part of his career Clapton was always associated with Gibsons – his championing of the Les Paul led Gibson to put it back into production in 1968, eight years after it had been discontinued. Following the emergence of Jimi Hendrix, though, Clapton switched to Fender Stratocasters, and these have been his main stage and studio electric guitars ever since. There's one nicknamed 'Brownie' that he used to play 'Layla', and was recently auctioned for $450,000 by Clapton to support his Crossroads drug rehabilitation charity. The most famous of his Strats, however, is the one Clapton nicknamed 'Blackie'. Blackie was put together by Clapton from three different Stratocasters. These came from a lot of six he bought in at the Sho-Bud music store in Nashville, Tennessee in 1970. Three of the six he gave away as presents to George Harrison, Steve Winwood and Pete Townshend. From the remaining three, he took the best parts and assembled Blackie. He played the guitar on stage and in the studio right up until 1987 when it was finally retired. Eager not to lose the sound of such a well-loved instrument, Clapton worked with Fender to produce The Eric Clapton Signature Stratocaster, a guitar designed to recreate Blackie, but with modern electronics. Particular enhancements have been made to the compression sound. A dedicated tone button allows the compression to fatten the sound considerably. At first the guitar was only available commercially in Ferrari Red, 7-Up Green and Charcoal Grey, but by 1991 Clapton relented and allowed the guitar to be commercially produced in black as well, much to the delight of Clapton wannabes.

Sunshine of Your Love

ALBUM: **DISRAELI GEARS (CREAM)**
SONGWRITERS: **ERIC CLAPTON, JACK BRUCE, PETE BROWN**
RECORDED: **ATLANTIC STUDIOS, NEW YORK**
PRODUCER: **FELIX PAPPALARDI**

This great opening riff is all played at the top end of the guitar neck on the bass strings. Play this riff on an electric guitar and turn the tone control right down to achieve that warm Clapton tone. Use down strokes with the plectrum, keep the notes evenly paced and practise moving between the three bass strings.

BASIC SONG RIFF

HERE'S HOW

1. This shows the ring finger at the D octave 12th fret, leaving your other fingers free to play notes on the lower frets.

2. Here the finger comes up to the A octave 12th fret of the A string. Use your middle and first finger on the next two notes.

3. Bring your ring finger up to the 10th fret of the E string whilst your first finger gets ready to play the 8th fret of the A string.

IT'S ALL ABOUT THE TONE

During the 1960s Eric Clapton not once but twice revolutionized the sound of the electric guitar, at least in Britain. It began with the album he made with John Mayall's Bluesbreakers. The unaccompanied guitar intro to 'All Your Love' made people jump out of their seats, it sounded so ferocious. The tone was reminiscent of Chicago blues players like Freddie King, but even more muscular. It was a tone Clapton achieved by plugging his Gibson Les Paul into an early Marshall Amp, a 1962 model 2x l2 Marshall combo fitted with a pair of KT66 power tubes, rather than the normal EL34s. Clapton played the combo full out and had the microphones placed across the room to pick up on the full force of this overdriven distorted sound.

The 1960s was a decade when technology was changing fast and by the time Clapton recorded with his next band Cream, his tone had changed too. He was playing a new Les Paul, after his previous one had been stolen; more significantly he was now playing through the classic Marshall 100-Watt amps with the new 4x12 Cabinets, stacked up in the studio. The result was louder than ever, but the better quality of the amplification meant that it was clearer too, offering a more melodic sound that aficionados soon dubbed 'woman tone'.

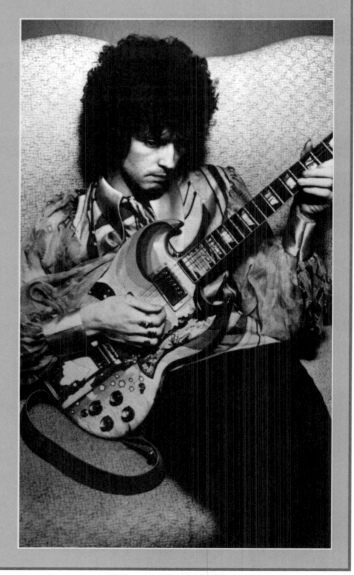

RIGHT: *Clapton's sound was influenced by the blues masters he listened to as a child, such as Robert Johnson and B.B. King. This picture was taken in 1967 during the recording of Cream's Disraeli Gears album in New York.*

Crossroads

ALBUM: **WHEELS OF FIRE**
WRITTEN BY: **ROBERT JOHNSON**
RECORDED AT: **THE FILLMORE WEST, SAN FRANCISCO**
PRODUCED BY: **FELIX PAPPALARDI**

A great rock blues riff that's really good fun to play. On the recorded version by Cream it's actually played quite fast, but you can slow it right down to practise getting the notes right. Set your amp to a dirty overdriven sound to achieve authenticity. Use your strumming hand to achieve a good bluesy boogie feel. Keep repeating the riff until you feel comfortable playing it at speed.

BASIC SONG RIFF

HERE'S HOW

1 Following the open A string the first finger plays the A note on the G string; this is quickly followed by an open G, then the A note again.

2 This shows a quick bend down on the C note of the A string. Practise moving from the bend quickly back into the riff.

3 Here the first finger covers the 2nd frets of the B and E strings. Strum these notes together in quick succession.

DOBRO

When Clapton came back from heroin addiction with 1974's *461 Ocean Boulevard* album, many long–time fans were aghast. For this was an album of laid-back songs with hardly a guitar solo to be heard. The dominant influence on his guitar playing was no longer Albert or Freddie King but Oklahoma singer-songwriter J.J. Cale. And much of the time Clapton was playing a Dobro!

A Dobro was about the least likely guitar-hero instrument you could imagine. It was invented in the 1920s by the Dopyera brothers at a time when guitarists were looking at ways of making their instruments louder so they could be heard in a swing band. The Dobro achieved this by incorporating a resonant aluminium cone and a steel body. The guitar is played horizontally and fretted with a steel bar ('a steel'), The result is a sound midway between blues bottleneck slide guitar and a pedal steel guitar. In fact, the introduction of first the electric guitar and then the pedal steel drove the Dobro almost out of existence by the 1940s; only the devotion of a handful of country and bluegrass musicians kept it alive. By the early 1970s, however, rock guitarists like Clapton and Ry Cooder were taking an interest in traditional country music, and found the unique sound of the Dobro fascinating. It's an indication of the instrument's growing popularity that, since 1993, Dobros have been manufactured by Gibson, who also produce signature editions endorsed by the virtuoso likes of Jerry Douglas.

RIGHT: *Eric Clapton's use of a particular guitar has an enormous commercial value for a company. Both Fender and C.F. Martin & Co. have honoured Clapton with signature models.*

Layla

ALBUM: **LAYLA AND OTHER ASSORTED LOVE SONGS**
WRITTEN BY: **ERIC CLAPTON, JIM GORDON**
RECORDED AT: **CRITERIA STUDIOS, MIAMI**
PRODUCED BY: **TOM DOWD**

Another very famous Eric Clapton riff, all played at the top end of the guitar neck. On the recorded version there are lots of multi-tracked guitars, but this tab will at least enable you to play the basic riff. You will need to practise to get the riff up to speed. Listen to the record to get the exact phrasing, and practise the fast phrases between the 10th and 13th frets.

BASIC SONG RIFF

HERE'S HOW

1 This shows the first finger at the 10th fret of the B string. Play this very fast hammer-on to the 13th fret with your little finger.

2 Here the riff goes up to the top E string. Play these notes at the 10th and 13th fret with your first and little fingers. Bend the highest note up.

3 This is the highest point of the riff at the 15th fret of the E string. Play this note with your little finger.

STEVIE RAY VAUGHAN

1954–1990
BANDS: **THE NIGHTCRAWLERS; DOUBLE TROUBLE**
HEIGHT OF FAME: **1970s**

In his short life Texas bluesman Stevie Ray Vaughan made a hell of a splash. He played guitar with David Bowie before becoming the first white musician to win a W.C. Handy Blues Instrumentalist of the Year award. Following his death in a helicopter crash, he has become a legend – a guitar player who married extraordinary technique with unbridled passion. At a time when the blues was slipping out of the consciousness of the average rock fan, Stevie Ray Vaughan kept the flame alive and in turn inspired a whole new generation of players.

RIGHT: *Stevie Ray Vaughan's dexterity with the electric guitar led some critics to make a comparison with Jimi Hendrix, such was his level of talent.*

Vaughan was born in Texas on 3 October 1954 at the Methodist Hospital. He was inspired to play guitar by his older brother, Jimmie. Leaving school at the age of 17, Stevie played in a series of rock bands before joining blues band The Nightcrawlers. At around this time, Stevie bought a battered '63 Stratocaster in Ray's Music Exchange in Austin. He named it 'Number One' (or sometimes 'First Wife') and this became his favourite guitar for the rest of his life.

The Nightcrawlers never quite made it, but Stevie persevered, playing a series of locally successful blues bands before forming his own group Double Trouble. A tape of the band playing live ended up in the hands of Mick Jagger, who invited them to play at a party for The Rolling Stones. This break led to Ray being hired by Bowie.

The Bowie connection raised Stevie's profile but what was even more pleasing was the success of *Texas Flood*, which was nominated for two Grammys. A string of hit albums followed. Unfortunately, along with the success came alcohol and drug problems which led to Vaughan going into rehab after collapsing on stage. Emerging sober, he recorded two more hit albums before his tragic death in a helicopter crash following a gig with Eric Clapton on 26 August 1990.

NUMBER ONE STRATOCASTER

Stevie Ray's favourite Stratocaster was one he bought in Ray's Music Exchange in Austin, Texas in his early years and nicknamed 'Number One'. This guitar was a battered 1963 model with a 1962 neck. Stevie Ray often said in interviews that he knew straight away that there was something special about it. 'I didn't even have to play it – I just knew by the way it looked that it would sound great. I was carrying another Strat and asked if Ray would like to trade. Thank God he did.'

Number One originally had a white pickguard and a right-handed tremelo bar. Stevie replaced the white pickguard with a black one and added 'SRV' lettering. In 1977 he added a gold left-handed tremelo – left handed to give him an upside-down guitar feel a la Jimi Hendrix. Eventually Stevie replaced the frets with Dunlop 6100 bass-style frets. These huge frets gave Stevie Ray the sustain he needed and helped during string bending. They were also helpful as he always used the thickest string sizes, ranging from .013 right up to .018.

Such strings are very hard on the fingers but if Stevie demanded a lot of his hands, he demanded even more of his guitar. Number One was severely abused during its lifetime with Stevie. On stage, Stevie Ray would kick it, pound it, rattle it, and hold it by the tremelo bar. Sometimes he would even bounce his guitar off a wall, catch it, and keep playing. The guitar finally had to be retired in 1989. Rumours suggested that it was buried with Stevie but in fact it's now in the possession of his brother Jimmie.

RIGHT *Stevie Ray's infamous 'Number One' guitar. It was much abused throughout its lifetime, but yielded the superb Stevie Ray sound.*

Pride and Joy

ALBUM: **TEXAS FLOOD**

SONGWRITER: **STEVIE RAY VAUGHAN**

RECORDED: **DOWN TOWN STUDIO, LOS ANGELES; RIVERSIDE SOUND, TEXAS**

PRODUCER: **DOUBLE TROUBLE, JOHN HAMMOND, SR.**

For this Stevie Ray Vaughan riff you'll need to tune down a semitone to get it to sound like the recorded version. It's a great blues intro which you can try and adapt and experiment with. Make that slide up from the 3rd fret to the 5th fret on the B string really ring out. It's a superb riff for practising your slides and bending note, and it also sounds good played slow or fast.

BASIC SONG RIFF

swing

HERE'S HOW

1. This shows the slide up from the 3rd to the 5th fret on the B string. Make sure you play the open E and let the notes ring out.

2. Here the picture shows the first finger at the 7th fret of the E string and the middle finger at the 8th fret of the B string.

3. The middle finger pulls this bend on the A note at the 2nd fret of the G string. Your middle finger can also play the following notes on the D string.

IBANEZ TUBE SCREAMER

An Ibanez Tube Screamer is an overdrive/distortion pedal, one which fattens and dirties up the sound of the guitar, making it ideal for blues playing. Its effect isn't as extreme as some: it allows the true sound of the guitar to come through. Most players use the device in conjunction with a tube amp to give it some extra power. The first Ibanez Tube Screamer to be manufactured was the green TS-808 overdrive pro in the late 1970s which followed on from the same company's regular overdrive pedals.

Stevie Ray Vaughan used both the early TS-808 and the later TS-9 Ibanez Tube Screamer stomp boxes in his career. The TS-808 is easily distinguished from the TS-9 by its small black knobs, smaller stomp button, white script on the housing, and darker green colour.

Stevie used the Tube Screamer as his primary distortion device. He employed it to add overdrive at the front end of his tube amps, and also to add a natural tube-like saturation and sustain to his lead. He believed that it particularly suited the tone of the Stratocaster, but would adjust his settings depending on which amp he was using. When he used smaller Fender amps that had natural overdrive, he used the TS set clean with the level up high to push the amp for more distortion. When he played through big clean amps he turned the drive up further in order to get the distortion from the Tube Screamer.

Today, the Ibanez Tube Screamer has become a coveted pedal and commands high prices, largely thanks to its association with Vaughan.

LEFT: *Stevie Ray Vaughan leans into a solo. His use of the Ibanex Tube Screamer generated the perfect 'dirty' blues sound.*

Scuttle Buttin'

ALBUM: **COULDN'T STAND THE WEATHER**
SONGWRITER: **STEVIE RAY VAUGHAN**
RECORDED: **THE POWER STATION, NEW YORK**
PRODUCER: **STEVIE RAY VAUGHAN**

This tab shows the three chords used at the start of ' Scuttle Buttin'' . The lead part is fairly difficult to master but these fast-flowing bluesy chords are great fun to play. You can also experiment with these chords and use them with other blues-based tunes, so try to incorporate them into your repertoire. Practise switching between these chords until you get the change smooth, then when you feel ready try using them to jam along with other musicians.

BASIC SONG CHORDS

E7♯9

A7

Bm7

HERE'S HOW

1

1 The first finger plays the D string, the ring finger plays the D and the little finger plays both 3rd frets on the B and E strings.

2 Here the middle finger plays the D string, the ring finger plays the B and the little finger plays the G note on the E string.

3 Start with the first finger on the A string, middle finger on the G, ring finger on the E and little finger on the B string.

3

2

JAZZ GUITARISTS

Jazz is one area of popular music where the guitar is less than all powerful. If you ask an average listener what the key rock'n' roll instrument is, they'll tell you it's the electric guitar. Ask what the key jazz instrument is, though, and they'll more than likely tell you it's the saxophone. However, the guitar is a versatile instrument and one that has a way of forcing itself to the fore. In the early days of jazz, if it was used at all, it was only to provide a basic rhythmic accompaniment, while these days, in the hands of musicians like Pat Metheny or Bill Frisell, it's a well-respected lead instrument. So, ask the question again in another 50 years or so, and maybe you'll get a different answer.

The absence of guitar from the beginnings of jazz is easy to explain. Jazz has its roots in the marching bands of New Orleans, which produced such founding figures as the legendary Buddy Bolden and the immortal Louis Armstrong, and which were dominated by brass instruments. Thus early jazz combos featured horns, which are loud instruments, plus bass and drums. An unamplified acoustic guitar simply couldn't make itself heard over such a line-up. Banjos, which have a slightly more ringing tone, were used occasionally, but were still hard for primitive recording devices to pick up on. It was only with the development of the microphone in the 1920s that the acoustic guitar – till then generally associated with classical or folk music – made its way into jazz.

The man largely responsible for its introduction was Eddie Lang, an Italian-American whose real name was Salvatore Massaro (and would hide behind the alias 'Blind Willie Dunn' when he recorded blues records, in a rare instance of a white musician having to pretend to be black rather than vice versa). Single-handedly Lang demonstrated that the guitar could be used in jazz not only as a rhythm instrument – the way banjos had been used in the past – but, given a well placed microphone, as a lead instrument too. Lang played the first single string guitar solos on record and worked with all the great names of early jazz – Louis Armstrong, Kid Oliver, Joe Venuti, Bix Beiderdecke and others. In 1932 he teamed up with the vocalist Bing Crosby, who was the first in his field to understand the technical implications of microphone recording for a singer. Sadly, a year into their partnership, in 1933, Lang died following a botched tonsillectomy.

JAZZ GUITAR GIANTS

A year later the next great jazz guitar virtuoso emerged, and, to general amazement, he was not an American but a French gypsy named Django Reinhardt. His 1934 recordings with the Hot Club of France were revelatory. Django brought in the influences of European classical and gypsy folk music and suggested new possibilities not just for jazz guitar but for jazz itself. Despite having only two functioning fingers on one hand, Django was a prodigious virtuoso and also a notable composer whose 'Nuages' remains a staple for any aspiring jazz guitarist.

Not all jazz guitarists were as flamboyant as Lang and Reinhardt, however. Freddie Green, for example, stayed with Count Basie for nearly 50 years and throughout that time he was content to be the mainstay of the band. Nicknamed Mr Rhythm, Freddie Green stuck valiantly to his task. Where other guitarists took to single-string soloing and then to the new electric guitars, Freddie Green stuck to the often unnoticed but invaluable job of keeping a beat as regular and as organic as a heartbeat. There are plenty of contenders for the greatest jazz lead player of all time, but there's only one for the title of the greatest rhythm player.

FAR LEFT: *Charlie Christian – one of the formative jazz guitarists. Guitars were not central to the origins of jazz music, but have steadily become more influential.*

ELECTRIC REVOLUTION

If Freddie Green is one of the great unsung heroes of jazz guitar, the next great innovator is one of the great what-ifs. Like Eddie Lang before him, Charlie Christian revolutionized jazz guitar. Christian's great innovation was again linked to technology. In this case that innovation was the advent of the electric guitar.

Christian wasn't the first jazzman to go electric; another jazzman, Eddie Durham, had done that, playing first with Jimmie Lunceford, and then alongside Freddie Green in the Count Basie Band, which was where Christian first encountered his playing. After seeing Durham play, Christian went out and bought himself an electric guitar, and within two years he was playing with Benny Goodman, and almost single-handedly writing a new vocabulary for his instrument. With the power of the electric guitar he was able to make the instrument swing like a horn; indeed many of the innovations Charlie Parker would come up with on the saxophone were at least partially anticipated by Christian's work with Goodman. Sadly, after just three years as a recording artist, Charlie Christian contracted TB and died in 1942. His small stack of recorded works are a jazz guitar treasure trove to rank alongside Robert Johnson's blues recordings.

PUSHING THE BOUNDARIES

Christian's innovations were immediately followed up by other guitarists. Another key player of the 1940s and 1950s was George Barnes, whose 1946 recording of 'Lover Come Back To Me', on which the guitar was the only solo instrument, backed by bass, drums and rhythm guitar, really pushed the boundaries forward and anticipated the work of the next great pioneer in the field, Tal Farlow.

Farlow was working as a sign painter when he heard Charlie Christian on the radio and promptly decided to take up the guitar. He taught himself how to play all of Charlie Christian's solos by listening to Benny Goodman records. He then moved to New York and played with the likes of Buddy deFranco, Artie Shaw and Red Norvo, before making a series of recordings under his own name in the 1950s that established him as one of the greatest jazz guitarists of all time. His innovations included a willingness to use the whole range of the guitar to play solo lines, and a fondness for chromatic chords, all coupled with extraordinary speed, a distinctly unorthodox technique and, of course, a continued adherence to the central jazz tenet that it don't mean a thing if it ain't got that swing.

The other great name of 1950s jazz guitar was Barney Kessel from Muskogee, Oklahoma. Another Charlie Christian disciple, he picked the opposite coast to Farlow and moved to Los Angeles, where he worked on the Marx Brothers live show as well as recording with Charlie Ventura, Roy Eldridge and Artie Shaw. From the mid 1950s on he concentrated on recording rather than touring and, while he was an avowed disciple of Christian, his career could hardly have panned out more differently. Christian's playing survives on only a handful of discs and was, initially at least, mostly an influence on fellow guitarists. Barney Kessel, by contrast, played on literally thousands of recordings and is probably more than any other individual, responsible for instilling the notion of the jazz guitar in the popular consciousness. In fact, he may be one of the most recorded musicians in the history of recorded music.

Not all jazz guitarists followed Christian's electric lead however. Charlie Byrd, a jazz guitarist who'd studied with the classical guitar legend Andres Segovia in the mid 1950s, began to play the concert (acoustic) guitar in a jazz setting. Byrd's first successes saw him incorporating classical influences into his playing, but the record that made him an international star brought in a more exotic influence, that of the Brazilian samba. In 1962 Charlie Byrd had

ABOVE: *Virtuoso jazz guitarist Django Reinhardt is pictured here jamming with Duke Ellington and his band in 1939.*

travelled to South America, and on his return to the US he recorded the classic *Jazz Samba* with Stan Getz, which became a huge hit with the wider public.

Popular though it was, the jazz samba movement was something of a passing craze. The next major innovator in jazz guitar was yet another Christian disciple, Wes Montgomery. After an apprenticeship spent playing rhythm guitar with the Lionel Hampton band, he formed The Wes Montgomery Trio and made a string of classic recordings between 1959 and 1963. Wes Montgomery's particular gift was for melodic improvization. He could make the most hackneyed jazz standard sound fresh. What marked him out to the casual listener, however, was the warmth of his sound, achieved by using his thumb rather than a pick, like almost all his predecessors.

So popular was this warm sound that from 1963 his records became increasingly oriented toward a mass market, full of orchestration and contemporary pop tunes. These recordings were more significant for their commercial success than for the musical qualities, and hardly go down well with jazz-guitar purists. However, they made Wes Montgomery a household name and helped elevate the guitar to a whole new level in American popular music. Wes Montgomery died suddenly of a heart attack in 1968. He left behind a legacy that included changing the guitar's place in popular culture. For the jazz guitarist who concentrates on his earlier work with the trio, he left an unsurpassed musical legacy. He also had an enormous

BELOW: *Pat Metheny is a leading modern Jazz guitarist, a musician with an accessible style who is not afraid of experimentation.*

influence on his contemporaries, including great melodic jazzers like Grant Green and Jimmy Raney.

By the time Wes Montgomery died in 1969 the electric guitar had been well and truly claimed by rock'n'roll, and for jazz guitarists that came after Wes the influence of Jimi Hendrix is often just as potent as that of Charlie Christian.

ROCK INFLUENCES

The first major jazz figure to take on board the influence of rock music was the great Miles Davis. From the late 1960s onwards his bands almost always included fiery lead guitarists, from John McLaughlin, who played with him on the epochal *Bitches Brew*, to Mike Stern and John Scofield, who accompanied him in his latter years.

Bitches Brew ushered in an era of jazz rock, which saw players crossing over from both sides of the musical divide. Rock guitarists like Frank Zappa and the Soft Machine's Allan Holdsworth became increasingly influenced by jazz, while jazz-schooled players from Larry Coryell to Sonny Sharrock found themselves incorporating rock dynamics into their technically complex playing. At its worst jazz rock would see technique being prized a long way ahead of creativity – as if all guitarists were locked in a battle to see who could play the most notes in the shortest period of time. At its best, though, if you return to Miles Davis' records like the aforementioned *Bitches Brew* and *In A Silent Way*, this was a period that opened up new possibilities for jazz guitarists, allowing them to step out of the overly polite formula that the success of Wes Montgomery and others had ushered in.

Not of course that the We Montgomery tradition simply died out. Instead it developed into what became known as jazz funk – essentially mellow dance music with a jazz feel. Notable players in this area were Earl Klugh, Robben Ford (another Miles Davis alumnus) Eric Gale and above all George Benson. A fine underrated guitarist in the Montgomery mould, and a smooth soulful singer, George Benson hit the big time with the multimillion selling *Breezin'* and never looked back.

In complete contrast to the smooth sound of Benson are those guitarists intent on pushing jazz to its sonic limits. These include the likes of Ornette Coleman's sideman James Blood Ulmer and the subtle experimentalist Bill Frisell.

Undoubtedly the most popular out and out guitarist in the jazz world today is Pat Metheny, a musician who takes his inspiration from jazz, classical and rock music, but has fused them all into a sound that can only be classified as Pat Metheny jazz guitar.

CHARLIE CHRISTIAN

1916–1942
BAND: **SESSION MUSICIAN**
HEIGHT OF FAME: **1930s**

Charlie Christian was the founding father and primary architect of the modern jazz-guitar style. He was the first major soloist on the electric guitar. Before Christian guitarists were predominately un-amplified acoustic musicians who were relegated to strict rhythm-guitar roles in an ensemble. With Christian the electric guitar became a distinct solo voice, equivalent to a saxophone, trumpet or clarinet, and capable of the same levels of expressiveness and intensity. Following Christian's initial appearance and short career, a school of disciples emerged – not only jazz players like Barney Kessel and Tal Farlow, but also blues and rock guitarists from T-Bone Walker to Scotty Moore, all of whom spread his influence far and wide.

RIGHT: *Charlie Christian was a pioneer in the field of electric jazz guitar in the blues, and as such cast an influence that reached up to the likes of Hendrix and Clapton.*

Charles Henry Christian was born in Bonham, Texas, on 29 July 1916. The young Charles took informal guitar lessons from his father and became serious about the instrument in 1933, when, along with his friend, T-Bone Walker, he took lessons from Ralph 'Big-Foot Chuck' Hamilton. Then in 1937 Christian bought his first electric guitar, probably a Gibson ES 150, and began to assemble the components of his horn-like approach. His distinctive sound soon made him a regional star and in July 1939, jazz producer John Hammond set up an audition with Benny Goodman. Christian was hired and relocated to New York City.

Charlie Christian's playing on tunes like 'Air Mail Special', 'Honeysuckle Rose', and 'Solo Flight' soon made him one of the biggest names of the swing era. By 1940 he was pushing the boundaries further, mixing with the new bebop musicians like Dizzy Gillespie and Thelonious Monk. Sadly he had always been troubled

by respiratory problems and on 2 March 1942 he died from tuberculosis. In a period of less than three years, Charlie Christian had emerged from total obscurity to produce a copious body of material which forever altered the course of guitar playing in jazz.

THE CHARLIE CHRISTIAN GUITAR SOUND

Charlie Christian is the man responsible for what we all now think of as the classic jazz guitar sound. Christian favoured Gibson arch-top hollow-body guitars, generally with f-holes, equipped with built-in electromagnetic pick-ups. The second important element was the amplification. Christian used Gibson EH (Electric Hawaiian) amplifiers, the EH 150 and the EH 185. Using this equipment with its combination of a pick-up in the neck position, a resonant hollow body and relatively small, not particularly powerful, amps, Christian achieved a thick, but clean, tone which was well suited to the single note lines of his impeccable solos.

CHARLIE CHRISTIAN'S GIBSONS

Charlie Christian's favourite guitar was the Gibson ES 150. Gibson announced the production of the first Electric Spanish guitar, the ES 150 in mid-1936 as 'Another miracle by Gibson – a true, undistorted tone amplified by electricity.'

One of its earliest fans was Count Basie's guitarist Eddie Durham who persuaded Charlie Christian to try one out. The rest, of course, is history and it wasn't long before the ES 150 became known to one and all as the 'Charlie Christian model'. Christian is known to have played at least three different ES 150s during his short career. The ES 150 was a non-cutaway acoustic with a carved spruce arch top and maple back and sides. It had a mahogany neck, a rosewood fingerboard and an ebony bridge.

The ES 150 was fitted with a single bar pickup, also now known as a 'Charlie Christian pickup', which was adjustable for height and could be tilted slightly. The pickup itself was close to the fingerboard, which gave the guitar

a deep bass-heavy tone. Christian adjusted the pickup closer to the body, away from the strings. This resulted in a warmer, mellow tone quality, with less output.

Christian also played the Gibson ES 250 guitar. Introduced in late 1939, this was basically an L-7 type with a larger, superior-grade 17in (43cm) body, inlays on the fingerboard, and a modified Charlie Christian pickup with a deeply notched blade to better balance the string response. Christian is thought to have played at least four of these models between 1939 and 1942.

LEFT: *Charlie Christian's Gibson guitars provided a clarity of sound essential for the basic early recording techniques.*

I Found a New Baby

ALBUM: **THE GENIUS OF THE ELECTRIC GUITAR**
SONGWRITERS: **SPENCER WILLIAMS, JACK PALMER**
RECORDED: **COLOMBIA STUDIOS, NEW YORK**
PRODUCER: **N/A**

All great jazz players can slip easily between complex chords and playing lead runs and scales. You can use this passage to practise this technique. Movement between the notes needs to be smooth and sound easy. Holding a 'chord shape' means you can play individual notes much more quickly. Make the shapes shown and practise moving between them. Try to make the pattern flow and sound easy so that your fingers begin to move naturally to the frets.

BASIC SONG RIFF

HERE'S HOW

1 Use your first finger on the A string and second finger on the G string. Use your ring and little finger on the D and B strings.

2 Slide up one fret to make this shape and practise forming the shape using first, middle and ring fingers – practise moving between these shapes.

3 Slip between the chord shape and single note section by using your little finger at the 7th fret of the B string on this part.

DJANGO REINHARDT

1910–1953
BAND: **QUINTET OF THE HOT CLUB OF FRANCE**
HEIGHT OF FAME: **1930s**

If the word 'genius' means anything perhaps it should refer to those whose talents are impossible to classify. Such a person was the gypsy guitarist, Django Reinhardt. Reinhardt was not a trained musician in the ordinary sense. He never learned to read and write – words or music. However, his instrumental technique was so unorthodox and his music so brilliant that it amazed fellow guitar players the world over. Almost all the great jazz guitarists of the second half of the twentieth century have acknowledged their debt to him. Some, like Joe Pass and Herb Ellis, have even recorded tributes to him.

RIGHT: *Django Reinhardt was actually one of a number of gypsy jazz guitarists making their presence felt in Europe during the 1930s, but he achieved fame through playing alongside the likes of Stephane Grapelli.*

Jean Baptiste 'Django' Reinhardt was born on 23 January 1910, in Liverchies, Belgium, but grew up in a gypsy camp outside Paris. He first studied violin, then proceeded to a banjo-guitar. By the time he was 13 he was good enough to play in Parisian dance halls, and in 1922 he began professional work. In 1928, however, he was the victim of a caravan fire, resulting in major damage to the first two fingers of his left hand. Despite this setback, Reinhardt managed to develop a revolutionary two-finger technique.

By 1930 Reinhardt was playing in public in Paris again and taking in the influence of American jazz musicians like Louis Armstrong, Duke Ellington and guitarist Eddie Lang. In 1934 he met violinist Stephane Grappelli, with whom he founded the Quintet of the Hot Club of France. The group achieved international acclaim within a year and recorded some 200 sides including such classic original compositions as 'Djangology', 'Minor Swing' and the international hit, 'Nuages' before World War II put their career on hold. After the war, Reinhardt toured the United States with

Ellington in 1946, where he played an amplified guitar for the first time, but the critics were dismissive of his work. Reinhardt returned to Europe, thoroughly disillusioned with the United States. Back in France he turned his musical interest to bebop, continuing to play an electric guitar. He died from a stroke at the age of 43 on 16 May 1953 in Fontainebleu, France.

DJANGO'S FINGERS

On the morning of 2 November 1928, Django was engulfed in a fire in the caravan in which he was living. He was taken to hospital where it was found that, amongst other terrible injuries, the two middle fingers of his left hand were welded together. After six months of constant treatment, the burnt flesh was moulded back into the shape of two fingers, but they were paralyzed and useless. Nevertheless, a doctor suggested to his relatives that they bring Django a guitar.

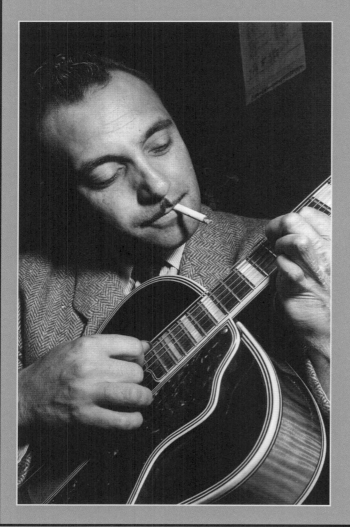

Overcoming terrible pain Django worked furiously with his left hand and finally managed to devise a new chording technique to compensate for the loss of the use of the fingers. He used his damaged third and fourth fingers to a limited extent on the first two strings and used the first and second left-hand fingers most of the time in single-note work. Most innovative, though, was the way in which he would play his octave passages on any two strings, with a 'damped' string in between, i.e., on first and third; second and fourth; third and fifth; etc., so as to avoid rushing up and down the fingerboard. His chromatic runs, meanwhile, if played in the first position, were fingered; or if played up the fingerboard, he would gliss them with one finger.

Inevitably, Reinhardt sought out unusual chord shapes using his damaged fingers. He also made extraordinary use of his good right hand. If you are lucky enough to see archive footage of Django, just watch and wonder: this is one guitarist whose style it could take a lifetime to emulate.

LEFT: *Reinhardt's hand injury led to his playing some unique chord progressions and distinctive melodies.*

Nuages

ALBUM: **VARIOUS COMPILATIONS**
WRITTEN BY: **DJANGO REINHARDT, JACQUES LARUE**
RECORDED: **VARIOUS RECORDINGS**
PRODUCER: **N/A**

This is a gorgeous tune played by the master of jazz guitar. Although you may not be able to accomplish some of Django's more dazzling runs, the tab shown here gives you the basic theme of 'Nuages' which you should be able to master with a little practice. To exercise fingers, practise ascending and descending runs on the B string as shown. Get used to moving between lead runs and chords with ease.

BASIC SONG RIFF

swing

HERE'S HOW

1 Starting at the 8th fret on the B string with your little finger, start the descending run using your ring, middle and first fingers.

2 Move from the descending run on the B string to this chord using all four fingers. Practise the run then form the chord straight after.

3 Play the B string with your first finger; your middle finger plays the G string, and your ring and little fingers play the A and D strings.

PAT METHENY

1954–
BAND: **PAT METHENY GROUP**
HEIGHT OF FAME: **1980s–90s**

Pat Metheny is the most influential jazz guitarist of modern times. His style looks backwards and forwards at the same time. On the one hand he comes out of the jazz tradition – he plays guitar almost like a horn player, with an extraordinarily loose, fluid style. On the other hand, he has constantly embraced new technology to become one of the great pioneers in using guitar synthesizers, from the 1980s onwards.

Pat Metheny was born into a musical family in Kansas City on 12 August 1954. Starting on trumpet at the age of eight, Metheny switched to guitar at age 12. By 15, he was working regularly with the best jazz musicians in Kansas City. He burst onto the international jazz scene in 1974, playing with vibraphone great Gary Burton, before releasing his first album, *Bright Size Life*, in 1975. Over the years, he has performed with artists as diverse as Steve Reich, Ornette Coleman, Joni Mitchell and David Bowie. He has been part of a writing team with keyboardist Lyle Mays for more than 20 years. His body of work includes compositions for solo guitar, small ensembles and large orchestras.

Metheny was one of the very first jazz musicians to treat the synthesizer as a serious musical instrument. He was also instrumental in the development of several new kinds of guitar, such as the soprano acoustic guitar, the 42-string Pikasso guitar, Ibanez's PM-100 jazz guitar, and a variety of other custom instruments.

He has won 15 Grammy Awards including an unprecedented seven consecutive Grammys for seven consecutive albums. His extraordinary popularity for a jazz artist has been cemented by his non-stop touring – Metheny has actually spent most of his life on tour, averaging between 120–240 shows a year since 1974.

RIGHT: *Pat Metheny is a major tour artist. He does not have just one single musical identity, but shifts styles according to the demands of his audience and musical genre.*

ROLAND GR300

Synthesizers appeared on the music scene during the late 1960s and early 1970s. These early models invariably used keyboards to control them, and thus it was only keyboard players who used them at first.

Soon the synthesizer manufacturers started work on designing a synthesizer that could be triggered by a guitar rather than a keyboard. Early models included the Arp Avatar and the Korg X911 but most of these units were severely flawed. Some did not allow string bending and others mis-triggered if you held a note too long, or in some cases if you didn't hold it long enough. This forced the guitarist to play very slowly and deliberately. Forget slides, harmonics, and even sloppy but spirited playing: if you couldn't play every single note clearly and directly, you might as well have turned the unit off.

BELOW: *Pat Metheny's studio collaborations have included the likes of jazz players such as Charlie Haden, Dave Holland, Roy Haynes and Ornette Coleman.*

Then came the Roland GR300. This was the first guitar synth that had the speed and accuracy of response to allow a guitarist to play like a guitarist rather than simply concentrating on cleanly triggering the module. It offered a range of processing options and the accompanying floor unit could be set to play root and harmonic duets. Pat Metheny was an early adopter. 'I just picked the GR300 up and I couldn't believe it, because it worked,' he told *Guitar Player* magazine, 'I could play all my kind of weird phrasings and it translated.'

Remarkably enough, after two decades of further technical innovation, Metheny still plays the GR300, and it remains one of the greatest guitar synths ever manufactured.

Travels

ALBUM: **TRAVELS**
SONGWRITERS: **PAT METHENY, LYLE MAYS**
RECORDED: **RECORDED LIVE IN DALLAS, TEXAS**
PRODUCERS: **PAT METHENY, MANFRED EICHER**

This is a lovely melody by Pat Metheny from the album Travels. *The individual notes should be picked with a nice clear tone; listen to the theme of the piece a few times to get the melody in your head. The melody is shown over two strings, so practise moving with ease between both. If you play along with the record try to improvise a few of your own notes within the theme.*

BASIC SONG RIFF

HERE'S HOW

1 Your little finger will play this 6th fret on the B string. Practice getting the phrasing exactly right with your picking hand.

2 Here your first finger plays the A note on the G string. Experiment with phrasing and your own notes when you play around this lovely theme.

ABOVE: *Pat Metheny's guitar style with the Pat Metheny Group is difficult to locate. While sitting recognizably in the category of jazz, it also makes incursions into the territories of funk, pop and easy listening.*

Phase Dance

ALBUM: **PAT METHENY GROUP**
SONGWRITERS: **PAT METHENY, LYLE MAYS**
RECORDED AT: **TALENT STUDIOS, OSLO**
PRODUCED BY: **MANFRED EICHER**

The tab for this riff calls for smooth interaction between the three highest strings (E, B and G). By playing two notes together on the B and G strings it gives the tune a lovely ringing quality. You can let your first finger do the work by covering all the notes at the 5th fret across all three strings. Practise your picking technique, switching between two notes on the B and G strings and single notes on the E string.

BASIC SONG RIFF

HERE'S HOW

1 Notice how the first finger covers all the notes at the 5th fret on all three strings. Get used to moving between double and single notes.

2 Use your middle and ring fingers for these notes on the B and G strings. This keeps the first finger free to cover single notes on the E string.

The whole riff is based around this pattern. Learn to play it fluently, speeding up as you get more comfortable and confident.

COUNTRY GUITARISTS

Country music in its earliest form is essentially the rural folk music of America, as brought over by settlers from Europe in general, and the British Isles in particular. There's no magical moment of beginning. Whether one considers an act like the Carter Family, recording in the 1920s, to be 'country' or 'folk', it's hardly a scientific distinction. Broadly speaking, one might say that the transition from rural singers entertaining their communities with renditions of folk songs to professional artists recording original material with its roots in the folk style is the transition from folk to country. By the 1930s, the success of acts like the Carter Family had put country music firmly on the musical map.

Just as the precise origins of country music are difficult to pinpoint, so too is the moment at which the guitar became a major instrument within it. The guitar had arrived in America with early European settlers, and gradually European guitar makers came to America and began building instruments there. They were still fairly rarefied instruments, however, until the Industrial Revolution of the late 1800s came along, and with it the technology to mass produce musical instruments, amongst them the guitar. Even then, however, the guitar was originally still seen as more suitable for classical music, as it didn't produce enough volume to compete with the fiddles and banjos popular with the folk-based string bands of the day. The appearance of the louder steel string guitars changed that a bit, but it was only the adoption of the guitar by black Southern blues players that really started to spark the instrument's popularity.

Gradually white musicians started trying the new instruments out and, by the early 1900s, quite a few white rural string bands featured guitars. Typical in this respect was one of the first significant country guitar players, Sam McGee, later to play in the band at the Grand Ole Opry. He learned about guitar picking from black railroad workers who played during their lunch breaks near his Tennessee home.

As folk musicians and string bands started developing the rudiments of what we would now recognize as country music, so the popularity of the guitar spread, helped hugely by the fact that cheaply produced models were appearing in the new mail order catalogues. The first major country music star was Jimmie Rodgers, 'the singing brakeman'. He played a guitar and provided a huge further boost to the instrument's popularity. Jimmie Rodgers helped sell many guitars in the late 1920s and early 1930s through his use of the instrument.

Gradually the first country guitar stylists began to emerge. First there was the Carter Family's Maybelle Carter. She developed her famous drop-thumb guitar style, as typified by her solo work on 'Wildwood Flower', providing the inspiration for generations of country pickers. Then came Karl Farr of The Sons of the Pioneers. His acoustic guitar playing began to show a distinct jazz influence, derived from players like Django Reinhardt. Soon country guitarists like California's Porky Freeman started to show levels of virtuosity only previously seen in the jazz field – as illustrated by Freeman's hit recording of 'Boogie Woogie on the Strings' or Zeb Turner's 'Zeb's Mountain Boogie'.

PICKING PIONEERS

Perhaps the definitive country music guitar style is the fingerpicking style, more particularly the syncopated Western Kentucky thumb and index finger picking style pioneered by Kennedy Jones. Jones himself used a thumb pick, but his style formed the basis for the picking of Ike Everly and Mose Rager, who in turn taught the style to the man who would bring it to a much wider audience, the great Merle Travis.

Travis was born in Rosewood, Kentucky, on 29 November 1917. He became fascinated with the playing of Everly and Rager and made a point of showing up whenever they performed in the area. Later he formed a group called the Drifting Pioneers who, in 1939, joined the musical staff at 50,000-Watt WLW Radio in Cincinnati. His abilities as a guitar soloist were obvious to the management, and he began playing on the station regularly, helping to spread the gospel of fingerpicking.

One such listener to WLW was the then 16-year-old Chet Atkins. Travis's playing immediately inspired him. In March 1944 Travis moved to Los Angeles, where he quickly found work as a sideman

FAR LEFT: *Scotty Moore was the guitar sound behind Elvis Presley, his talent immortalized in records such as ' That' s All Right' and ' Jailhouse Rock' .*

with the western swing bands of Porky Freeman and Ray Whitley. In 1945 he recorded his first disc under his own name. The following year his disciple Chet Atkins made his own debut with a recording of *Guitar Blues*, a laid-back, late night blues recorded on electric guitar.

By 1946, Travis' reputation was such that he'd begun doing session work for Capitol Records, the major independent label on the West Coast. In March, Travis was signed to Capitol as a solo artist. He soon began taking guitar breaks on his records, which became extremely influential. By the late 1940s Travis was established as the nation's top country guitarist. Chet Atkins' popularity was, meanwhile, only just beginning to build after his 1947 signing to RCA Victor.

POSTWAR DEVELOPMENTS

A number of other fine guitarists developed in the wake of Travis, among them the Texas-based singer and band-leader Hank Thompson, who had a string of hits in the 1940s and 1950s. He became an excellent fingerpicker, following Merle Travis's example to the point of having Gibson custom-build him a Super 400 electric.

By 1950 Chet Atkins had started to come out from Travis's shadow. He'd had a solo spot on the Opry as Red Foley's guitarist around 1946, and then worked as a sideman until Steve Sholes signed him to RCA in 1947. It soon became apparent, however, that Chet's direction was more oriented towards instrumentals, and RCA began to release instrumental sides by him which quickly became popular.

It's no doubt largely because he recorded as an instrumentalist that Chet Atkins is a better known as a guitarist than Merle Travis. While Travis was concentrating on a career as a singer, songwriter and guitarist, Chet was almost exclusively recording instrumentals. While Merle was recording vocals for Capitol, Chet was racking up numerous instrumental hits and gaining a strong reputation for his work in the fledgling Nashville recording scene. Chet also developed a style that differed significantly from Travis as he started to incorporate the influences of non-country instrumentalists like Les Paul and Django Reinhardt.

Many other guitarists began to be influenced by Atkins, not just in the US but also in the UK, where he was a big influence on the likes of George Harrison and even Ritchie Blackmore. Many of them were unaware how much actually came from Merle Travis. One American guitarist who learned from both Chet and Merle was Scotty Moore. When, in the summer of 1954, Scotty started working with Elvis Presley on his epochal Sun sessions, and Presley recorded his version of 'That's All Right', Moore's accompaniment was straight out of Travis and Atkins' style book.

Other legendary early rock stylists heavily influenced by the Atkins/Travis style included Eddie Cochran, Duane Eddy, and, above all, Jerry Reed, who took the Atkins/Travis styles a quantum leap ahead. Reed began as a rocker, recording for Capitol, but by the 1960s he was a Nashville studio musician with his own style of fingerpicking. Where Travis used the thumb and index finger almost exclusively, and Atkins used his thumb and at least two other fingers, Reed used them all.

Chet Atkins and his followers are all, of course, associated with the electric guitar, typically the big bodied Gretsches. However, acoustic stylists, generally working in the acoustic style that was starting to became known as bluegrass, were making their own innovations. Lester Flatt developed a dynamic guitar style full of bass runs while playing first with Bill Monroe's Blue Grass Boys and then with Earl Scruggs. Other fine bluegrass guitarists included The Stanley Brothers' George Shuffler, who crosspicked his instrument, and guitarist Doc Watson who came up with the idea of fingerpicking fiddle tunes.

In the mainstream of country music, however, it was electric guitars that ruled the roost by the 1960s. Scotty Moore's innovations were developed by the Telecaster-playing James Burton working successively with Ricky Nelson, Elvis Presley and Emmylou Harris. Bakersfield country star Buck Owens was another fine electric stylist, as was his regular lead player Don Rich, and fellow Bakersfield legend Merle Haggard's guitarist Roy Nichols. Glen Campbell was another artist best known as a singer, but actually a formidable guitarist as well, who played on a huge number of 1960s country and pop hits, even working with Phil Spector.

ABOVE: *Chet Atkins – aka 'Mister Guitar' – was a pioneer of what is today known as the Nashville sound, and he helped the spread of popular country music.*

BELOW: *One of the guitars that created country – Maybelle Carter's Gibson L-5 archtop was amongst the finest instruments available in the 1920s.*

In the 1970s country got a shot in the arm as the outlaw movement rejected the 'countrypolitan' blandness of much Nashville fare. The outlaws – Waylon Jennings, Willie Nelson and others – wanted to give the music some rock 'n' roll attitude and, of course, that meant turning up their guitars. Waylon Jennings' aggressive Telecaster came to the forefront, as did that of the British guitar hero Albert Lee, when he was drafted in to take over James Burton's role with Emmylou Harris's Hot Band. The Telecaster remained the country guitar of choice well into the 1980s, thanks to the likes of Dwight Yoakam's guitarist Pete Anderson and the session ace Jerry Donohue. By the turn of the decade, acts like the internationally massive Garth Brooks, with his lead-guitar player James Garver, were leading county music and country guitar playing right into the mainstream.

During the 1990s, perhaps as a reaction to the new popular country, acoustic country had something of a revival, considerably inspired by Willie Nelson's distinctively jazzy approach on the one hand and the technical bluegrass flash of players like Tony Rice and Ricky Skaggs on the other. These days, country music finds itself at a point where it's looking backwards and forwards at the same time, with guitar players studying the approach of Merle Travis and Maybelle Carter, then figuring out how to take it to the next stage.

SIGNATURE GUITARS

Jimmie Rodgers appears to have been the first country singer to have a guitar model named for him, when Weymann created their 'Jimmie Rodgers Special' model in 1930. This started a trend. As country music began to develop stars, so the manufacturers used their success to sell more guitars. In 1932 a WLS National Barn Dance singer, 'Arkie the Arkansas Woodchopper', had Martin guitars build him one of their large D-2 'dreadnought' guitars with a herringbone wood trim. It became the classic Martin D-28. The following year his fellow Barn Dance star, Gene Autry, had Martin build him an elaborate pearl inlaid version that became the D-45. And while these were top-of-the-range instruments, there was also an obvious market for cheap instruments that bore a star's endorsement. So Sears Roebuck began marketing its inexpensive 'Gene Autry' guitars in the 1930s, and these were the first guitars many young future guitar stars owned. The practice has continued to flourish ever since and today Martin Guitars manufacture signature models endorsed by a whole range of country stars from Johnny Cash to Willie Nelson, as well as historical models replicating guitars used by the likes of Hank Williams and even Gene Autry.

FINGERPICKING

The basic fingerpicking style (known as the 'choke' style) consists of the right-hand index finger picking out the melody while the thumb, usually equipped with a pick, plucks out a constant alternating bass accompaniment. The net result is a self-contained, rich, varied sound that gives the illusion of a lead and rhythm guitar being played simultaneously. Talented players have introduced their own individual variations of the basic style to create a personal sound. Merle Travis, for instance, would also brush the fourth, third, and second strings with the thumb on the upstroke while muting the strings with the right hand so as to create a percussive accompaniment. On occasion, Travis would add even more variety by interjecting a single-string melody.

The earliest fingerpicking styles evolved slowly, handed down from guitarist to guitarist in the Appalachian regions. One of the first influential guitarists from this area was a black bluesman from Louisville, Kentucky, named Sylvester Weaver, allegedly the first blues guitarist to ever record. His 1924 recording of 'Smoketown Strut' demonstrates the basic elements of what we have since come to think of as country fingerpicking. His intricate style led his label to dub him 'the man with the talking guitar'. The same tag would be given to Merle Travis in later years.

Another black guitarist, Arnold Schultz, may have had an even greater impact on the development of Kentucky fingerstyle. Though segregation was the norm back then, Western Kentucky seemed surprisingly open-minded to musical integration, and Schultz was a favourite at white square dances where he met and influenced, among others, a young Bill Monroe. Kennedy Jones was another guitarist influenced by Arnold Schulz. He in turn influenced Mose Rager and his long-time friend Ike Everly (father of Don and Phil), two former coalminers who started playing together in the early 1930s, and influenced many budding guitarists, among them the great Merle Travis.

MAYBELLE CARTER

1909–1978
BAND: **THE CARTER FAMILY**
HEIGHT OF FAME: **1930s–40s**

'If it hadn't been for Mother Maybelle,' said music writer Hazel Smith, 'Jimi Hendrix might have been a banjo player.' This may be overstating the case a little, but there is no doubt that Maybelle Carter is one of the absolute pioneers in modern guitar playing. Every folk and country guitarist owes something to Maybelle Carter and most realize as much. Most blues and rock guitarists also owe her something as well, but hardly any of them appreciate it.

Maybelle Carter, playing with the Carter Family, single-handedly introduced the guitar as a lead instrument in country music. She took an instrument solely used for rhythm and basic chord accompaniment, and by devising her own technique for playing a bass-string melody accompanied by brushed chords on the treble strings, brought it to the forefront of popular music, a position it has held ever since.

Born Maybelle Addington in Nickelsville, Virginia, in 1909, Maybelle Carter grew up in a rural, mountain-dwelling family that spent much of their time playing music for social reasons. By the age of 12 she was known as a fine instrumentalist. In due course she formed a group, The Carter Family, along with her cousin Sara and her husband A.P. Carter, eventually coming to the attention of the Victor Talking Machine Company.

The recordings made by the Carter Family were an immediate hit and Maybelle used her first royalty check to purchase a Gibson L-5 archtop, the best model available from Gibson at the time, costing the then astronomical sum of $250. Armed with this new guitar, Maybelle helped the Carters to record a repertoire of folk and country songs that became the bedrock of American folk music – including the likes of 'Little Darling Pal of Mine', 'Keep on the Sunny

RIGHT: *Maybelle Carter (centre) with The Carter Family. Armed with Gibson guitars, Carter helped lay the foundations of modern bluegrass and country.*

Side', 'Wildwood Flower' and 'Will the Circle Be Unbroken?'

After the Carter Family dissolved as a group, Maybelle eventually formed a band with her daughters, Helen, Anita and June, which revived the original Carter Family's music in the late 1960s. Mother Maybelle, as she was known to the world, died in 1978.

GIBSON L-5

When Maybelle Carter bought her Gibson L-5 archtop in 1929, it cost proportionally as much as a new car today. However, it was an extremely sound investment, as she used the Gibson L-5 for nearly every recording and personal appearance for the next ten years. While on tour with The Carter Family in the 1950s, Elvis Presley would often borrow the Gibson from Carter when he broke a string on his own guitar.

The Gibson has a 16in (40.6cm) wide body, narrow snakehead peghead, maple neck and ebony fingerboard with white binding and dot inlay. It was originally set with banjo pegs, but Maybelle customized the guitar over the years with replacement tuners, pickguard and tailpiece.

Following Maybelle's death the guitar remained in the care of her family. It was loaned to the Country Music Hall of Fame in 1998 but was reclaimed in 2004 and put up for sale. Billed as the most important guitar in the history of popular music it was put on the market by Gruhn Guitars of Nashville with the extraordinary price-tag of $575,000. The uncertain fate of the guitar made national headlines and a local philanthropist eventually stepped forward making a $1,000,000 donation to the Hall of Fame in order to keep the guitar on public display.

LEFT: *Maybelle Carter's Gibson L-5 archtop has become almost an icon in the country music community.*

Wildwood Flower

ALBUM: **WILDWOOD PICKIN'**
SONGWRITERS: **A.P. CARTER**
RECORDED : **RCA VICTOR STUDIOS, CAMDEN, NJ**
PRODUCER: **JEFF ZARAYA**

This intro sounds best played on an acoustic guitar. It is played on the bass strings, which establishes the rhythm before the chords come in. Although in the same key on the recorded version the tune is actually played on the high strings, but either way it sounds great. Maybelle Carter also used the hammer-on technique on the D string. Practise mixing hammer-ons with straight picked notes on the bass strings.

BASIC SONG RIFF

HERE'S HOW

1 Use your middle and ring finger for the move from B note on the A string to C note. Make those intro notes punchy and solid.

2 This is the hammer-on played with the middle finger on the D string, make sure you play the open G string straight after the hammer on.

3 For the final note of the intro the ring finger plays the G note at the 3rd fret of the E string. Repeat this until you feel comfortable.

CHET ATKINS

1924–2001
BAND: **SOLO ARTIST**
HEIGHT OF FAME: **1950s–60s**

Unusually for an instrumental virtuoso, Chet Atkins was also an enormously influential producer. In fact it's fair to say that without Chet Atkins' production skills and musical vision, country music may never have crossed over into the pop charts in the 1950s and 1960s. During those decades, he helped create the Nashville sound, a style of country music that owed nearly as much to pop as it did to honky tonks. At the same time he was a consistently sensational guitar player, a musician who combined the complexity and technique of jazz with a country-pop sensibility. Simply put, he was as classy as popular guitar playing gets.

RIGHT: *Chet Atkins earned the label ' Mister Guitar' on account of his exceptional talent with a country tune, and he is one of history's most recorded instrumental artists.*

He was born on 20 June 1924 in Lutrell, Tennessee. He didn't begin his musical career by playing guitar. Instead, on the recommendation of his older brother, Lowell, he began playing the fiddle. However, Chet soon became attracted to the guitar, and at the age of nine he traded a pistol for a guitar. Atkins learned his instrument rapidly, inspired by Merle Travis, becoming an accomplished player by the time he left high school in 1941.

After years playing live as a backing musician, word of his prowess reached Nashville, where RCA boss Steve Sholes made Atkins the studio guitarist for all of the RCA studio's Nashville sessions in 1949. The following year, Mother Maybelle and the Carter Sisters hired him as a regular on the Grand Ole Opry. While he worked for RCA, he played on many hit records and helped fashion the Nashville sound. In 1953 the label began to issue a number of instrumental albums that showcased Atkins' considerable talents. Not only did his records sell well, he designed guitars for Gibson and Gretsch; the popularity of these models continues to the present day. Atkins' career continued

to prosper. He became manager of RCA's Nashville division and, while his own recordings dwindled in popularity in the 1970s, his reputation revived again in the 1990s following duet albums with the likes of Jerry Reed and Mark Knopfler. During his career he received 11 Grammy awards and nine CMA Instrumentalist of the Year honours. He died of cancer in 2001.

CHET ATKINS' COUNTRY GENTLEMAN

Given that he was not only a musician but also a business-savvy Music Row executive, it's hardly surprising that Chet Atkins was one of the first guitarists to have his own signature model guitar put into production. The guitar in question was the 1958 Gretsch Country Gentleman. The Country Gentleman is considered by many to be one of the holy trinity of 1950s Gretsch guitars, along with the 6120 and White Falcon. The other two may be more eye-catching but the Country Gentleman, as its name suggests, has an elegance (and some would say playability) the others lack. The fact that George Harrison often played one doesn't hurt, either.

The Gentleman was released in 1958, after considerable input from Atkins, and it was placed between the 6120 and Falcon in price. Originally it had a 43cm (17in) single cutaway body with fake f-holes inlaid into the mahogany-finished maple top. The closed body was a concession to Atkins, who was constantly hounding Gretsch to produce a semi-hollow guitar with a solid block through the centre, like Gibson's ES 335, in order to get more sustain and less feedback. Some early 1960s Gentlemen also appear with real f-holes, though.

Gretsch kept on making the guitars, albeit with regular modifications, until 1978 when Atkins jumped ship to Gibson, taking the name with him. Gretsch renamed the guitar the Country Squire and kept on producing them, while Gibson now make a considerably different guitar under the Country Gentleman name. Atkins' own Gentleman recently came onto the market at a very reasonable $50,000.

LEFT: *The Gretsch Country Gentleman was Atkins' formative instrument until he moved to Gibson in 1978.*

Mr Bojangles

ALBUM: **ALMOST ALONE**
SONGWRITER: **JERRY JEFF WALKER**
RECORDED: **CA WORKSHOP; CREATIVE RECORDING, NASHVILLE**
PRODUCER: **CHET ATKINS**

The best way to play this lovely tune is to form a chord shape like a C; this will enable you to pick out the notes fluently with your picking hand. The tune is based around the chords C, Am and G7. Keep your fingers clear of the stings not being played. Keep notes clean and separate. Use up and down strokes with your plectrum, as this will help to increase speed.

BASIC SONG RIFF

HERE'S HOW

1 This is the C chord minus the use of the E (6th) string. Pick out the notes shown in the tab from this shape.

2 Let the middle finger come up from the 2nd fret D string to play the B note on the 2nd fret of the A string.

3 For the third chord (A minor) use your middle finger at the second fret of the D string, ring finger at the second fret of the G string and first finger at the first fret of the B string.

SCOTTY MOORE

1931–
BAND: **ELVIS PRESLEY; SESSION MUSICIAN**
HEIGHT OF FAME: **1950s–60s**

Scotty Moore is one of the great pioneers of guitar. As Elvis' original guitarist he was at the heart of the fusion of country and R&B that came to be known as rockabilly. His sharp, memorable licks and keen sense of when to play hard and when to pull back complemented Presley's vocals perfectly. Also, while Moore is generally associated with Elvis' early material – particularly the groundbreaking recordings made at Sun Studios – he actually continued to play on the records until the late 1960s, with much of his finest work appearing on early RCA classics like 'Hound Dog' and 'Jailhouse Rock'.

RIGHT: *Scotty Moore is pictured here with the king of rock 'n' roll himself, Elvis Presley. Many critics believe that his recording of 'That's All Right' with Elvis in 1954 inaugurated the era of rock and pop.*

Scotty Moore was born Winfield Scott Moore III on 27 December 1931 on a farm near Gadsden, Tennessee. He began playing guitar at the age of eight, learning from family and friends. He enlisted in the US Navy in 1948, serving in Korea and China. Discharged in January 1952, Moore settled in Memphis. He formed a country band, recording a single for Sun Records in the spring of 1954. Soon afterwards the band met up with another hopeful, one Elvis Presley, and on 5 July 1954 the team recorded 'That's All Right', the first great rockabilly record.

At first, Moore and Black were almost equal partners with Presley, and Moore also became Presley's first manager. Soon, however, it became clear who the star was, but Scotty remained Elvis' favourite guitarist, integral to his sound. Moore's ongoing work with Elvis finally came to an end in the late 1960s, although he did make an appearance on stage with the King on his heralded 1968 television comeback special. After a long layoff, Moore returned to the stage in the 1990s, performing with Carl Perkins and on Elvis tribute shows.

THE GUITAR THAT CHANGED THE WORLD

The Gibson L5 has been one of the great success stories of guitar history. Originally manufactured in the early years of prohibition, it is still in production – albeit in an updated version – over 80 years later. Along the way it has helped revolutionize folk and country (thanks to Maybelle Carter), jazz (courtesy of Wes Montgomery) and rock 'n' roll (pioneered by Scotty Moore).

Originally manufactured in 1922, the Gibson L5 is the precursor of the modern archtop guitar. It was the first archtop to feature f-holes, which allowed it to project through the horn-dominated bands of the day. Its strong, full, warm sound was an immediate and overwhelming success. As electrification was introduced, Gibson began to manufacture electric – or semi-acoustic – versions. Scotty Moore traded his previous guitar, a Gibson ES 295, for one of these on 7 July 1955 at Memphis' legendary music store, the O.K. Houck Piano Co.

Why the change? Scotty said it was simply 'because the workmanship was just so much better in the L5 – and, of course, it cost more too.' It was first used to record 'Mystery Train' and featured on most of the subsequent RCA recordings until January 1957 – that's to say it was used to create the absolute, original classics of rock 'n' roll. Moore played it live as well, using a custom-built Echosonic amplifier by Ray Butts, which he acquired around April 1955, and which gave him the ability to perform live with his signature slap-back echo sound.

LEFT: *Scotty Moore was an ideal guitarist for Presley. His openly expressed philosophy of 'keep it simple' meant his guitar did not compete with the singer but still provided the driving force of rhythm and melody.*

Mystery Train

ALBUM: **VARIOUS COMPILATIONS**
SONGWRITERS: **HERMAN PARKER JR, SAM C. PHILLIPS**
RECORDED: **SUN STUDIO, MEMPHIS**
PRODUCER: **SAM C. PHILLIPS**

This riff makes use of the bass strings to create a lovely driving country rock sound. The riff starts with a hammer-on and is based around the chords E and A. The way Scotty Moore and the rhythm section play this tune actually makes it sound like a train. Try to achieve a rhythm like a train moving along. Practise picking bass notes before hitting chords. Use this technique on other intros.

BASIC SONG RIFF

HERE'S HOW

1 The middle finger is used for the hammer-on intro; this leaves the first finger ready to play the A flat note on the G string.

2 For this section play the open strings to form a chord. The first and middle fingers are holding the notes on the G and D strings.

3 The rhythm really gets going here. Use the first finger to cover all notes at the 2nd fret.

ECHOSONIC AMPLIFIER

The key to Scotty Moore's revolutionary guitar sound was his use of echo. And that echo was down to a remarkable amplifier, the Echosonic. Scotty first heard Chet Atkins using one. 'I don't remember the name of the record,' he recalled years later, 'but I heard one of Chet's instrumentals on the radio. His guitar had the same slap, but it was a little bit different to what I was used to hearing Sam Phillips do with us. I said, "Damn. How is he doing that?"'

After some investigation, Scotty located the man who made the amplifer, an accordion player and electronics whiz named Ray Butts, and bought one. It was only the third one ever to be made. The 25-Watt amp featured a built-in tape delay system that gave Scotty his slapback echo sound. Unlike studio echo, he was able to use this live as well. Legend has it that in his early days of performing with Elvis the PAs that venues supplied were often so inadequate that sometimes Elvis himself would plug his mic into the Echosonic as well.

The first recording Moore used his new purchase on was 'Mystery Train' in July 1955. Thereafter, he employed it on every subsequent recording and performance throughout his career with Elvis, right up until their last appearance together, the 1968 NBC-TV special. Moore used it again when he returned to performing, but has since retired it for fear of damage in transit.

Only 68 Echosonics were ever produced, all handmade one at a time. Apart from Scotty and Chet Atkins, other owners included Carl Perkins and Roy Orbison. Scotty still has his to this day.

LEFT: *Scotty Moore on stage with Elvis during a 1950s TV show performance. Moore worked with Elvis through to the late 1960s.*

Heartbreak Hotel

ALBUM: **VARIOUS COMPILATIONS**
SONGWRITERS: **TOMMY DURDEN, MAE BOREN AXTON, ELVIS PRESLEY**
RECORDED: **RCA STUDIOS, NASHVILLE**
PRODUCER: **STEVE SHOLES**

This is a great tune to practise your rock 'n' roll licks on. The slower pace means you'll be able to use this tune to build up speed for faster songs. The solo shown on the tab is at the top of the neck and sounds great against a rock 'n' roll rhythm section. Use your ring and little fingers to slide up to the 12th fret to create a nice rock 'n' roll sound.

BASIC SONG RIFF

HERE'S HOW

1. Slide into the riff playing both E and B strings at the 12th fret. Practise this slide, as it's used a lot in rock 'n' roll.

2. Hold your first finger back ready to play the 10th fret on the E string. Keep in mind the rhythm to help you with your timing.

3. Accentuate the last two notes on the E string. All great guitar solos are tunes in their own right, so listen for the melody.

FOLK GUITARISTS

Folk music is notoriously hard to define, partly because different people use the term to refer to wildly different types of sound. Perhaps the most generally accepted definition is that folk music is the music of the people, passed down through the generations and performed as part of the life of a community, rather than as a commercial undertaking. However, even if you take this definition as a starting point, it can still include a huge variety of music – delta blues, Appalachian mountain music, bluegrass, Celtic or English traditional music, gospel music, union songs, traditional music from Africa, Asia, and other parts of the world.

On the other hand, there are plenty of people who use the term 'folk music' to mean 'anything that's played on the acoustic guitar'. It's a definition that allows all sorts of artists to be bracketed as 'folk'. The result of all this is that anyone from an earnest singer-songwriter through a 1960s protest singer to a 1920s sharecropper might be described as a folk musician. Believe it or not, they don't all play the guitar the same way!

Well, this is isn't the place to debate the rights or wrongs of such definitions. Instead we'll endeavour to give you a brief outline of some of the principal guitar styles that might be described as 'folk'.

THE AMERICAN TRADITION

First off, we'll look at the guitar styles that have developed out of American traditional music, particularly country and blues. Two of the key influences on folk guitar playing both came up in the same area at the same time. Both Elizabeth Cotten and Rev. Gary Davis were born in the last decade of the 19th century in the Carolinas, and both played in the ragtimey, two-finger Piedmont style, but with strikingly different results. Cotten's playing combined elements of all the different music that was in her family – rags, dance tunes, hymns and parlour songs.

Her simple fingerpicked style provided the model for 1950s folk-boomers to learn from.

Cotten's influence was largely felt at second hand thanks to the adaptation of her style by commercial folk singers like Peter Paul and Mary. The Rev. Gary Davis was rather more of a star in his own right. His complex style, with its mix of ragtime and gospel influences derived from Blind Blake, had a more direct influence on the folk-boomers, with songs like 'Candy Man' and 'Cocaine Blues' becoming coffeehouse standards.

Another blues-based guitarist who had a powerful influence on folk music was Leadbelly. Leadbelly's trademark 12-string acoustic playing had a rhythmic drive that was to prove a huge influence on folk musicians to come. In particular, it influenced Leadbelly's regular associate, the pivotal figure in pre-1960s American folk, Woody Guthrie. Guthrie in turn would influence all the guitar-playing folk protest singers to come, from Pete Seeger and Ramblin' Jack Elliott to Bob Dylan and his whole legion of imitators. Woody Guthrie adapted old folk tunes as the settings for new lyrics which protested against poverty, injustice and bigotry, and he constructed simple, durable guitar parts to go with them. His goal was not to impress listeners with guitar wizardry, but to encourage them to pick up their own guitars, sing their own songs or pass his own songs along.

During the 1940s and 1950s this style made its way into the pop charts, with the gentle folk recordings of The Weavers and The Kingston Trio. In the 1960s, though, a huge boom in interest in folk music amongst college kids led to a whole range of more experimental new talents emerging. There was Ramblin' Jack Elliott who could swing from the Woody Guthrie style 'Roll in My Sweet Baby's Arms' to the Rev. Gary Davis-like 'Railroad Bill'. Or there was the expert fingerpicking of Dave Van Ronk, adding new sophistication to his interpretations of Leadbelly classics. Joan Baez, meanwhile, inspired a generation of young women to try their hand at folk guitar.

BRITISH ARTISTS

On the other side of the Atlantic the guitar took a little longer to be accepted as an appropriate instrument for folk music. The traditional instruments for British folk music were more likely to be concertinas or fiddles, or even banjos, than guitars. All that changed with the skiffle boom of the 1950s. In a rough counterpart to the American

ABOVE: *Woody Guthrie was a key figure in the development of American folk music, pre-dating and inspiring the 1960s generation of singer-songwriters which included Bob Dylan and Joan Baez.*

folk boom, skiffle consisted of white teenagers dong their best to impersonate Leadbelly.

One of these young skiffle guitarists was Martin Carthy, and as his interest turned to British folk music, so his immersion in the possibilities of the guitar as a folk instrument developed. Over the succeeding 50 years Carthy managed to more or less invent what is now seen as English folk guitar playing, characterized by spare fingerpicking and rock-solid thumb attack. It's a style of accompaniment that's both remarkably propulsive and sensitive to the demands of the song.

Other notable guitarists who appeared in Carthy's wake include Nic Jones, a gifted artist whose career was sadly cut short by a car accident that left him unable to play or sing, and the Scottish legend Dick Gaughan. Gaughan favours a flatpick and his best work is heard on his interpretation of classic folk ballads like 'Willie O'Winsbury' or 'Craigie Hill', involving a stunning integration of chordal accompaniment and fiery melodic work. He's also one of the finest interpreters of Celtic dance tunes, using the flatpick technique. His guitar ornaments can mimic fiddle bow skips or even bagpipe squawks. Like Carthy he regularly experiments with alternate tunings, for instance using EADEAE or EAAEAE to imply pipe drones under the melody.

Fine Irish folk guitarists include Paul Brady, whose 1970s recordings show him incorporating double-course technique into his flatpicking style, adding a rawness and urgency, and the Bothy Band's Mícheál Ó Domhnaill. Ó Domhnaill is probably the most widely imitated Irish guitarist. He built a unique style around DADGAD and establishes wonderfully interlocking rhythms and counter-rhythms.

BELOW: *Folk music is not necessarily about traditionalism. John Fahey was known for his acoustic experimentation, and his popularity underwent a resurgence with the musical avante garde during the 1990s.*

INSTRUMENTAL FOLK

All the folk guitar players mentioned so far essentially use the guitar as an accompaniment, albeit often a very elaborate one. During the 1960s, however, a new school of folk guitarist emerged who concentrated on purely instrumental work. These players, unsurprisingly enough, tend to be the ones who have lifted the style into new levels of technical virtuosity.

The pioneer in this direction was John Fahey, who started recording in 1959. Fahey took traditional blues and country acoustic guitar licks and used them to create a kind of American primitive classical music. Being a composer became the defining aspect of his music, as for many of his successors, who describe themselves as guitarist-composers. Among the first of these was Robbie Basho, who began his recording career on Fahey's own label. He was in some ways even more influential on the current crop of New Age guitarist-composers, with his love of Eastern music.

Another guitarist to debut on Fahey's label was Leo Kottke, who took the Fahey/Basho idea, and succeeded in bringing it to a mass audience. His 1969 album *Six- and 12-String Guitar* is arguably the most influential guitarist-composer record ever made. Increasingly, since the 1970s the development of instrumental guitar music in the US has inclined towards New Age. This shift began to pick up momentum in the 1980s with the success of Windham Hill Records with guitarists like Alex de Grassi, whose effortless flowing arpeggios and relaxed style really came to define New Age guitar, as did that of label mate Michael Hedges, with his prodigious two-hand tapping techniques.

BLUES EXPERIMENTATION

While the Windham Hill and Takoma artists were redefining fingerstyle guitar in the States, something similar was happening on the other side of the Atlantic. The British counterpart to John Fahey was another experimentalist named Davey Graham. Graham's album *Folk, Blues And Beyond* mixed traditional English folk with blues and North African influences to stunning effect. He was also one of the first British guitarists to experiment with alternate tunings, especially the enormously influential DADGAD.

Graham's disciples included John Renbourn and Bert Jansch, two fine guitar players who briefly teamed up in the group Pentangle. Renbourn's style is ornate, bringing influences from pre-Baroque English styles. Bert Jansch is a spikier guitarist. Heavily influenced by Graham's discovery of DADGAD, Jansch is a brilliant finger-stylist whose influence is not merely apparent in the likes of Donovan, but on the acoustic work of Jimmy Page as well.

All of these schools of folk guitar playing have their adherents, but perhaps the most influential of all are the ones we don't even think of as guitarists, or at least not as guitarists first and foremost. These are the 'folk' singer-songwriters who began to appear during the late 1960s, spearheaded by Paul Simon, Joni Mitchell and James Taylor. They may not have inspired people to become guitar virtuosos, but to do something arguably more important: to pick up the guitar in the first place.

ALTERNATE TUNINGS

So why do so many folk guitarists, from Joni Mitchell to Davey Graham, delight in using alternate tunings? Well perhaps the real question is why on earth standard guitar tuning is standard? After all the standard EADGBE tuning is actually based on a pretty strange combination of a major 3rd and four perfect 4ths, which makes some chords pretty difficult to play. The reasons for its adoption are partly historical, to do with the development of the instrument out of the lute, partly mechanical, as it doesn't place too much stress on any of the strings, and partly just luck, that this particular tuning happens to be the one that has stuck. Once a standard has been established, it makes everyone's life easier to stick with it. Plus once you've got a guitar tuned one way it's a considerable hassle to keep retuning it for different songs, particularly when playing live (assuming you don't have a guitar roadie waiting to supply you with any one of a dozen guitars kept in different tunings).

However, it's a mistake to let that put you off, as experimenting with tunings opens up a whole world of options, and they're not just for experts either. In fact it's a lot easier to play the basic chords in some alternate tunings.

The most common alternate tunings are what are known as open tunings, in which the open strings of the guitar are tuned to form a simple chord: thus the strings of the open C tuning form a C major chord, the strings of the open G tuning form a G major chord, etc. Invariably, this makes it easy to play in the 'natural' key of the tuning.

Another common use of open tunings is to play the open strings as drones. This is an easy way to create unusual chordal combinations and interesting sustained tonal clusters. They are also a big help when you are playing bottleneck or slide guitar, since you can place the slide at any fret and play a full six-string chord. Similarly, harmonics have extra possibilities in open tunings. You can play a full six strings of harmonics at the 12th, 7th and 5th frets.

Other options include tunings based on those of other instruments such as the mandolin, the cittern and the oud, which can produce some truly innovative sounds. Another option is to try out regular tunings, in which the strings are tuned uniformly up the fretboard. This allows chord forms to be moved up and down the fretboard like a normal bar chord, and also sideways across the fretboard, allowing even a novice guitarist access to a whole range of chords with minimal variation in fingering.

If the idea of retuning still intimidates you, maybe you should consider a MIDI guitar controller. With the flick of a button you can change the tuning of all six strings; and suddenly the possibility for experimentation is endless.

FLATPICKING

The two main styles of picking in folk guitar are known as fingerpicking (which is discussed in the country chapter) and flatpicking. Basically flatpicking is the technique of playing a guitar with a flat pick (or flat plectrum) rather than with fingers, finger picks, or a thumb pick. The plectrum is a thin sliver, generally made of plastic, nylon or tortoiseshell, and using it brings significantly different tones out of a steel-string guitar.

Both fingerstyle and flatpicking styles emerged in the early part of the century when musicians realized the guitar was capable of being more than simply a rhythm instrument. The term 'flatpicking' originated with early lead acoustic guitar players in traditional country and bluegrass music who started using plectrums. Some of the flatpicking pioneers included Don Reno and Bill Napier in bluegrass music, Django Reinhardt and Eddie Lang in jazz music, and the Delmore Brothers, the Blue Sky Boys, Jimmie Rodgers and Hank Snow in country music.

During the 1960s and 1970s the flatpicking technique became more widespread as the lead guitar became more prominent in bluegrass, folk and traditional music. Major exponents of the style include the likes of Doc Watson, Clarence White, Tony Rice and Norman Blake. The basic technique involves holding the plectrum with only your thumb and index finger to play the lower notes, while picking the upper notes with your middle and/or ring fingers. The most popular style of guitar for flatpicking is definitely the dreadnought, the larger style acoustic as manufactured by Martin. This is partly down to tradition and partly due to their bass response, making them the ideal guitars for bluegrass, which involves plenty of rhythm playing behind a string band.

BELOW: *Nick Drake was a quintessentially British folk guitarist, and is known for his highly unusual tunings.*

JOHN FAHEY

1939–2001
BAND: **SOLO ARTIST**
HEIGHT OF FAME: **1960s**

John Fahey is a guitarist who spent 40 years treading his own path. Like many of his contemporaries growing up in America in the 1950s, he was entranced by rediscovering the pre-war country and blues pickers. Few others, however, dipped into their work in such detail or succeeded in turning those influences into something equally mysterious and profound.

Some aspects of his guitar playing are almost self-consciously 'traditional', but Fahey's playing showed that fingerpicking techniques derived from country and blues could also be used to incorporate elements from Indian music and even touches from modern classical composers like Bela Bartok. It's a combination that the rest of the world is still catching up with.

Fahey was born on 28 February 1939, in Washington, D.C. The young Fahey developed a diverse musical taste embracing, pop, modern classical, and Episcopalian hymns. In his early teens Fahey bought his first guitar, a Silvertone, for $17, and began to try to play all the different kinds of music he loved. Increasingly he became drawn to American folk music.

He made his first album in 1959, giving himself the jokey pseudonym 'Blind Joe Death'. Through the early 1960s his albums steadily became more ambitious, taking in Eastern influences and stretching out to 20-minute improvisations, thus anticipating the experimentation of groups like The Grateful Dead. He also employed a whole range of unusual guitar tunings. He ran his own label, Takoma, until the 1970s, releasing records by protégés like Leo Kottke. In 1986 he contracted Epstein-Barr syndrome, a long-lasting viral infection, and the illness led to a downturn in his career. However, his work enjoyed a revival in the 1990s, and Fahey returned to recording and performing to considerable acclaim before his death in 2001.

RIGHT: *John Fahey returned to the live music scene in the 1990s, and is pictured here at a New York City gig in 1997.* City of Refuge, *his current album at the time, demonstrated his ongoing experimental fusion of folk and blues.*

AMERICAN PRIMITIVE

John Fahey's own name for his singular guitar technique was American Primitive. It's an atmospheric phrase that does indeed get to the heart of the Fahey project. Essentially, Fahey began by deconstructing the unschooled but remarkably complex playing of men like Robert Johnson or Charlie Patton and applying it to very different musical styles. He achieved this through the use of what is more commonly known as fingerstyle guitar. This is based on the strong right-hand techniques used by pioneering delta blues players coupled with alternate tunings.

Taking the picking first, the key is the syncopation, and in Fahey's playing this was often applied to unusually slow tempos. Thus Fahey might have played a three-note chord on the treble strings and moved in half steps up and down the neck of the guitar while the thumb kept alternating on open strings. However, while in jazz playing a chromatic move like this would be done at lightning pace, Fahey might dwell on each half step for a measure or two before moving on. Meanwhile the right hand would be offering a ragtime-like syncopation. The result of this, in Fahey's playing, would be to add the kind of dissonance you might find in Bartok to traditional American fingerpicking: American primitivism in action.

As for the tunings, Fahey would employ a whole range from the relatively familiar open G (DGDGBD) and open D (DAD#FAD) to the distinctly unusual open C (CGCGCE), open D minor (DADFAD), open G minor (DGDGBflatD) and C drone (CCCGCE).

LEFT: *Alongside being a musical eccentric – factory noises and trains featured in some of his recordings – Fahey was known to be a difficult and reclusive character, as unique as his music.*

The Yellow Princess

ALBUM: **THE YELLOW PRINCESS**
SONGWRITER: **JOHN FAHEY**
RECORDED: **SIERRA SOUND LABORATORIES, BERKELEY**
PRODUCERS: **SAMUEL CHARTERS, BARRET HANSEN**

This intro uses a fingerstyle technique to pick out notes on bass and high strings. Practise playing fingerstyle to improve your sound; there is a vast repertoire of folk tunes and instrumentals like this lovely John Fahey piece that you will be able to play once you have fully mastered this style of playing. Use your thumb to pick out notes on the bass strings. Learn to keep in time whilst playing in this style.

BASIC SONG RIFF

HERE'S HOW

1 Shows the B and A flat notes on the B and G strings, hold down both notes together ready for your picking hand to play them.

2 Note the thumb ready to play the E open string and the first and middle fingers ready to play the other notes in the tune.

NICK DRAKE

1948–1974
BAND: **SOLO ARTIST**
RECORDED: **LATE 1960s–EARLY 1970s**; HEIGHT OF FAME: **1990s–PRESENT**

As a person, the increasingly legendary British singer-songwriter Nick Drake was elusive, almost impossible to pin down. The same goes for his guitar playing. His friend and string arranger Robert Kirby once commented that while most distinctive guitarists have plenty of imitators, Nick Drake hardly has any.

RIGHT: *Nick Drake was a talented, if vulnerable, folk guitarist. His first guitar was purchased for £13, and many of the songs he wrote while at Cambridge University would be heard on* Five Leaves Left.

The reason why? 'Perhaps because it's so damn difficult.' Not only was Nick Drake fond of unusual tunings (which he never wrote down), he was also given to fantastically intricate fingerpicking patterns. It's this maverick originality that made Nick Drake one of the most brilliantly individual of all British guitar players.

Nick Drake was born in what was then Burma on 19 June 1948. His family returned to England when he was two and he went to Marlborough public (private) school when he was 13. While he was there he started playing the guitar and writing songs. From school he went on to Cambridge University and while still a student landed a recording deal with Island Records and top producer Joe Boyd. This team would put out two albums, both now regarded as classics. The first album, *Five Leaves Left*, was full of delicate guitar work and wonderfully complementary, very English string arrangements. The second, *Bryter Layter*, continued in the same vein, and when it failed to sell Drake was crushed. His final album, *Pink Moon*, produced by Drake and John Wood, was a sparse, dark record performed almost entirely solo. It was released in 1972 but, like its predecessors, failed to be a commercial success. Drake relapsed into a depression which was to last on and off till his tragic death in November 1974 following an overdose of sleeping pills. Since that time, his popularity has steadily grown, as subsequent generations have discovered the singular talents of a man sadly ignored by his own generation.

River Man

ALBUM: **FIVE LEAVES LEFT**
SONGWRITER: **NICK DRAKE**
RECORDED: **LONDON, UK**
PRODUCER: **JOE BOYD**

This is a gorgeous tune which sounds lovely strummed or picked. It requires a change of tuning to CGCFCE. Be careful to avoid breaking strings when you change the tuning. The diagram shows the first two chords in the song. Another chord used in the song is A flat. Try singing the vocal melody as you practise moving between these chords and add the A flat chord.

BASIC SONG CHORDS

C

Cm

HERE'S HOW

1 The first finger is on the 2nd fret of the G string, ring finger on the 4th fret of the B string and the middle finger plays the E string.

2 Try your first finger on the 2nd fret of the G string, your middle finger and ring fingers on the 3rd frets of the B and E strings.

LEFT: *Nick Drake was a remarkable musician who saw little commercial success during his short life. These photographs were taken by Keith Morris, the only professional lensman known to have photographed Drake during just three sessions, one for each of his albums.*

USEFUL CHORDS: A

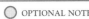

O OPEN STRING	X DO NOT PLAY THIS STRING ○ OPTIONAL NOTE
① INDEX FINGER	② MIDDLE FINGER ③ RING FINGER ④ LITTLE FINGER

A

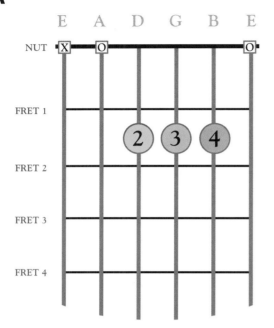

Your middle finger should play the 2nd fret of the D string, your ring finger plays the 2nd fret of the G string and your little finger plays the C# note at the 2nd fret of the B string.

A Minor

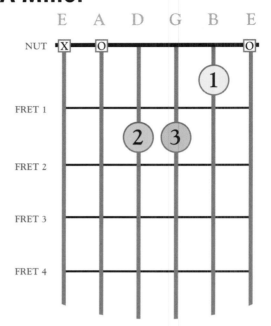

Let your index finger play the C note at the 1st fret of the B string, your middle finger play the 2nd fret of the D string. Your ring finger should play the 2nd fret of the G string.

A 7

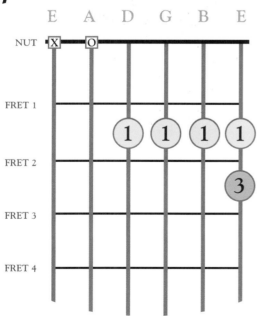

Use your index finger across the 2nd frets of the E,B,G and D strings only, then use your middle or your ring finger, whichever feels most comfortable, to play the G note at the 3rd fret of the top E string.

A Major 7

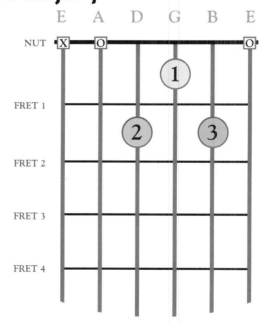

Use your index finger to play the 1st fret of the G string, your middle finger to play the 2nd fret of the D string and your ring finger to play the 2nd fret of the B string.

A Flat Major 7

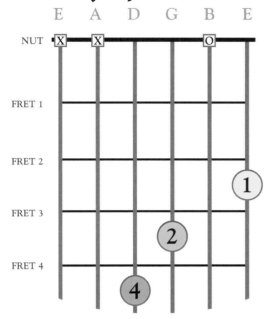

Use your index finger to play the 3rd fret of the top E, your middle finger to play the 4th fret of the G string, and your little finger to play the 5th fret of the D string.

A Minor 7

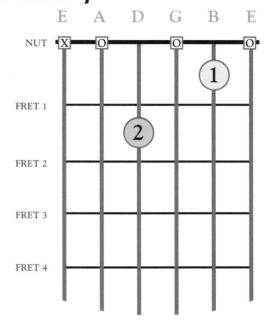

Let your index finger play the 1st fret of the B string and your middle finger play the 2nd fret of the D string. You should play all the other strings, except the bottom E, open.

A 6

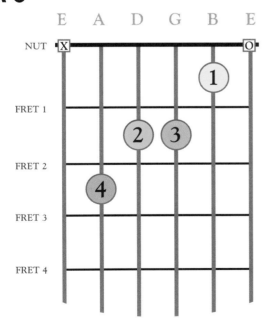

Use your index finger to play the 1st fret of the B string, your middle finger to play the 2nd fret of the D string, your ring finger the 2nd fret of the G string and your little finger to play the 3rd fret of the A string.

A 9

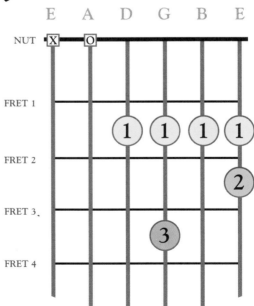

Use your index finger across the 2nd fret of the E,B,G and D strings, your middle finger on the 3rd fret of the top E, and your ring finger on the 4th fret of the G string.

USEFUL CHORDS: B

B

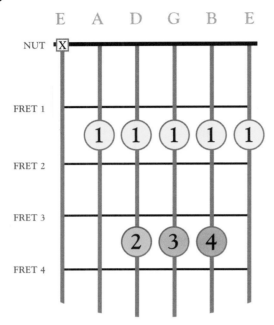

The 2nd fret of the E, B, G , D and A strings are played with your index finger. Middle finger plays 4th fret of the D string, ring finger plays 4th fret G string and little finger plays 4th fret B string.

B Minor

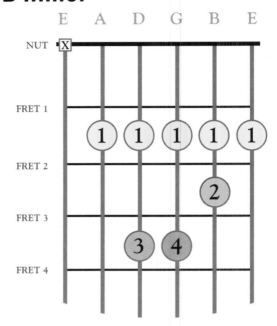

The index finger plays E,B,G,D and A strings at the 2nd fret. Middle finger plays 3rd fret of the B string, ring finger plays 4th fret of the D string and little finger plays 4th fret of the G string.

B 7

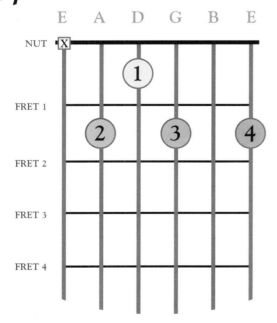

Your index finger plays the 1st fret of the D string, middle finger plays the 2nd fret of the A string, ring finger plays the 2nd fret of the G string and your little finger plays the 2nd fret of the top E.

B Major 7

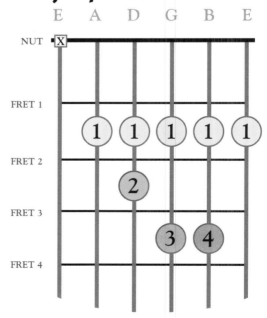

Let your index finger cover all 2nd frets of the E,B,G,D and A strings. Middle finger plays the 3rd fret of the D string, ring finger plays the 4th fret of the D string, and little finger plays the 4th fret of the B string.

B Flat

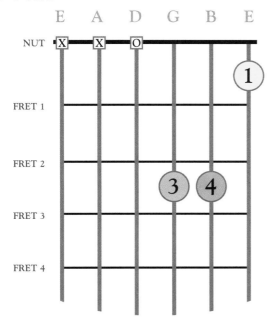

Let your index finger play the 1st fret of the E string and your ring finger play the 3rd fret of the G string. Finally let your little finger play the 3rd fret of the B string.

B Minor 7

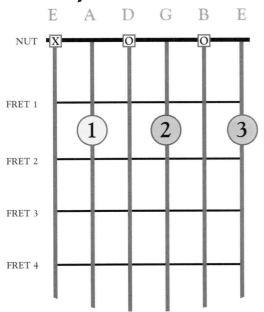

Use your index finger to play the 2nd fret of the A string, your middle finger to play the 2nd fret of the G string and your ring finger to play the 2nd fret of the top E string.

USEFUL CHORDS: C

C

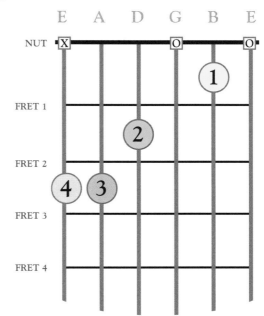

Your index finger plays the 1st fret of the B string, your middle finger the 2nd fret of the G string and the ring finger plays the 3rd fret of the A string. Playing the 3rd fret of the E string is an option.

C 7

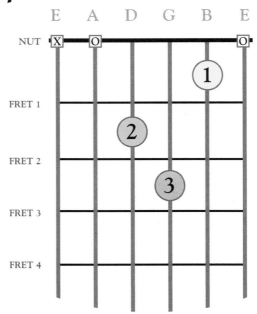

Use your index finger to play the 1st fret of the B string, your middle finger to play the 2nd fret of the D string and your little finger to play the 3rd fret of the G string.

C Minor

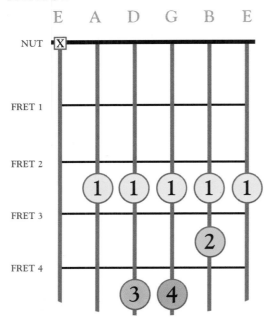

Your Index finger plays the 3rd fret of the E,B,G,D and A strings, your middle finger plays the 4th fret of the B string, your ring finger plays the 5th fret of the D string, and your little finger plays the 5th fret of the G.

C

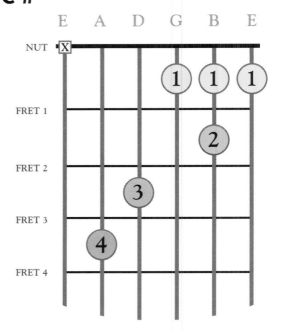

Let your index finger cover all 1st frets of the E,B and G strings, your middle finger play the 2nd fret of the B string, your ring finger play the 3rd fret of the D string and your little finger play 4th fret of the A string.

C Major 7

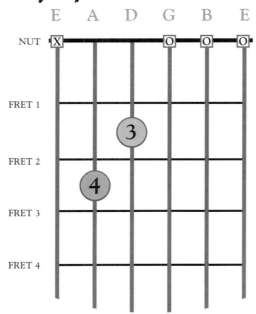

To play this chord you can either use your index and middle finger or ring and little finger, use whichever combination feels best. Play the 2nd fret of the D string and 3rd fret of the A string.

C 6

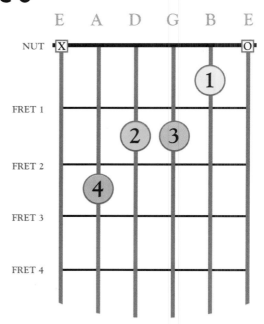

Use your index finger at the 1st fret of the B string, middle at the 2nd fret of the D string, ring finger at the 2nd fret of the G string and little finger at the 3rd fret of the A string.

USEFUL CHORDS: D

C Minor 7

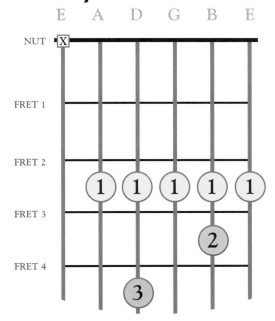

Use your index finger to cover all 3rd frets of E,B,G,D and A strings. Your middle finger plays 4th fret of the B string and your ring finger plays 5th fret of the D string.

C 9

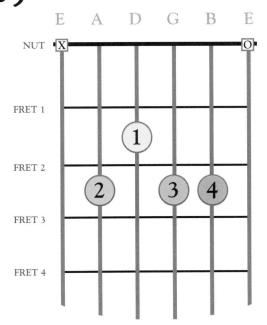

Your index finger should play the 2nd fret of the D string, your middle finger the 3rd fret of the A string, your ring finger the 3rd fret of the G string and your little finger the 3rd fret of the B string.

D

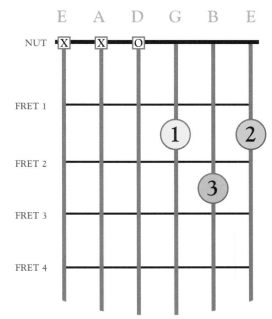

Use your index finger at the 2nd fret of the G string and your middle finger at the 2nd fret of the top E, leaving your ring finger to play the 3rd fret of the B string.

D 7

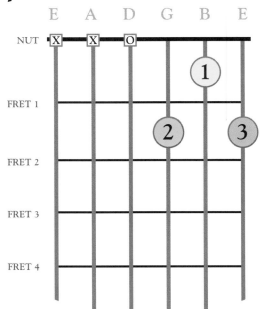

Let your index finger play the 1st fret of the B string, your middle finger play the 2nd fret of the G string, and your ring finger the 2nd fret of the top E string.

D Minor

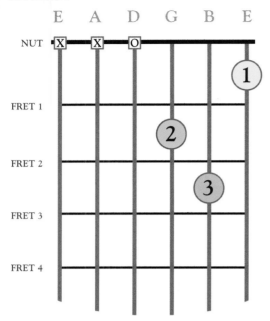

Let your index finger play the 1st fret of the top E string. Your middle finger should play the 2nd fret of the G string and your ring finger should play the 3rd fret of the B string.

D Minor 7

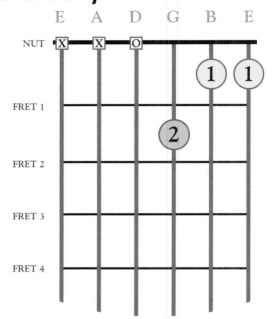

Let your index finger play the 1st frets of the top E and B strings, your middle finger play the 2nd fret of the G string. Include the D string which is played open.

D 6

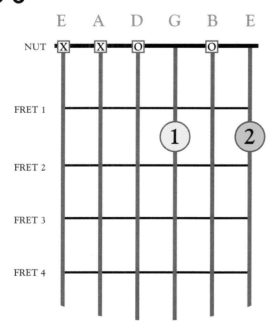

For this chord you can use either your index and middle finger or middle and ring fingers to play the 2nd fret of the G string and top E string.

D 9

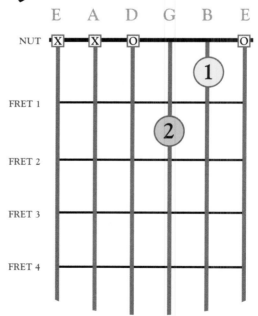

This is an easy one! use your index finger on the 1st fret of the B string and your middle finger on the 2nd fret of the G string. The D string and the top E should play out open.

USEFUL CHORDS: E

E

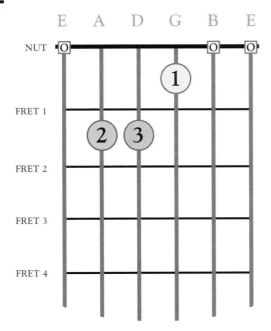

For the E chord your index finger should play the 1st fret of the G string, your middle finger should play the 2nd fret of the A string and your ring finger should play the 2nd fret on the D string.

E Minor

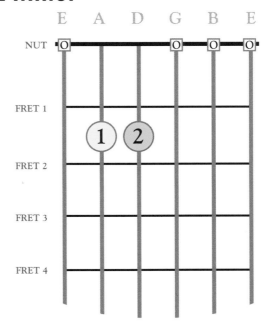

Your index finger plays the 2nd fret of the A string whilst your middle finger plays the 2nd fret of the D string. You can use the middle and ring fingers instead, if that feels more comfortable.

E 7

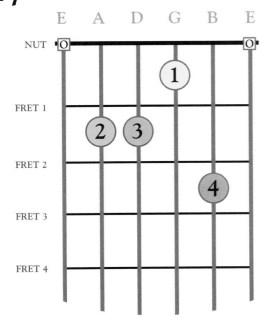

Let your index finger play the 1st fret of the G string, your middle finger play the 2nd fret of the A string, your ring finger play the 2nd fret of the D string and your little finger play the 3rd fret of the B string.

E Major 7

Let your index finger play the 1st fret of the D string, your middle finger play the 1st fret of the G string, and your ring finger play the 2nd fret of the A string.

E Flat

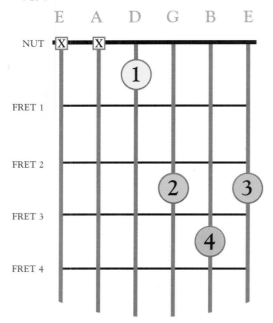

Your index finger should play the 1st fret of the D string, your middle finger the 3rd fret of the G string, your ring finger the 3rd fret of the E string and your little finger the 4th fret of the B string.

E Minor 7

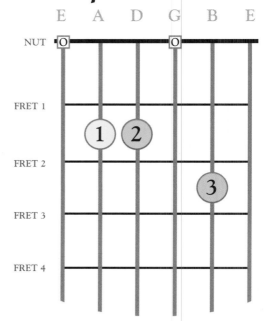

Let your index finger play the 2nd fret of the A string, your middle finger should play the 2nd fret of the D string and your ring or little finger should play the 3rd fret of the B string.

E 6

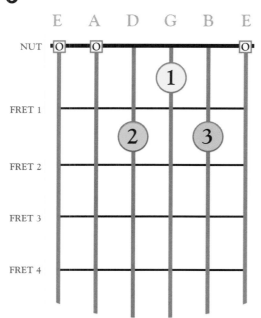

Use your index finger to play the 1st fret of the G string, your middle finger should play the 2nd fret of the D string, and your ring finger should play the 2nd fret of the B string.

E 9

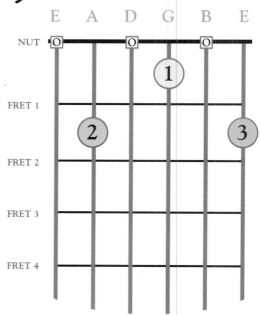

Let your index finger play the 1st fret of the G string, your middle finger should play the 2nd fret of the A string and your ring finger should play the 2nd fret of the top E string.

E Flat Major 7

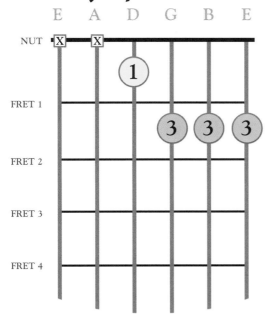

Use your index finger at the 1st fret of the D string, then let your ring finger (or middle finger if that feels more comfortable) cover the 3rd frets of the E,B and G strings.

USEFUL CHORDS: F

F

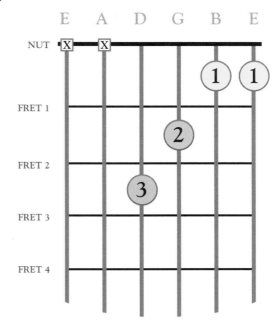

Your index finger should play the 1st frets of the E and B strings, with your middle finger playing the 2nd fret of the G string and your ring finger playing the 3rd fret of the D string.

E Flat Minor 7

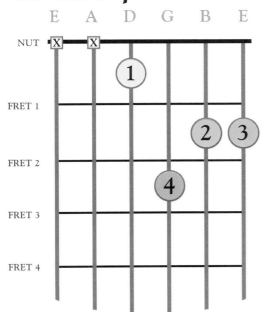

Use your index finger to play the 1st fret of the D string, your middle finger to play the 2nd fret of the B string, your ring finger to play the 2nd fret of the E string, and your little finger to play the 3rd fret of the G string.

F 7

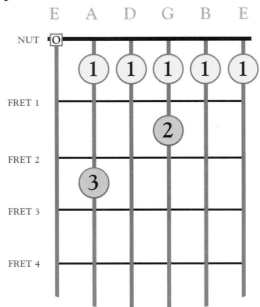

Let your index finger play across all 1st frets of the E,B,G,D and A strings, let your middle finger play 2nd fret of the G string and your ring finger play the 3rd fret of the A string.

F Minor

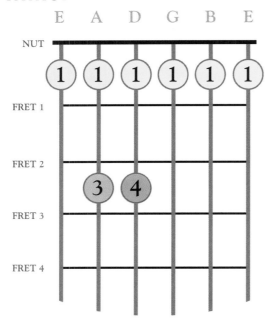

Use your index finger to play all strings at the 1st fret. Use your ring finger to play the 3rd fret of the A string and your little finger to play the 3rd fret of the D string.

F Major 7

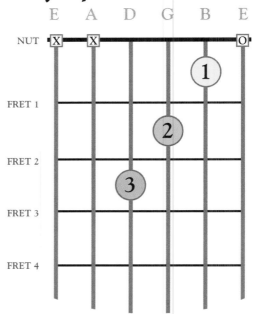

Use your index finger to play the 1st fret of the B string, and your middle finger to play the 2nd fret of the G string. Finally use your ring finger to play the 3rd fret of the G string.

F

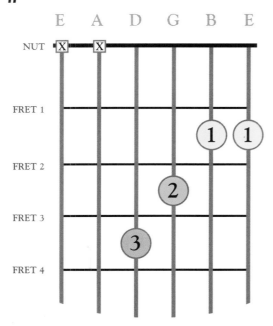

For the F# chord let your index finger play the 2nd frets of the E and B strings. Your middle finger plays the 3rd fret of the G string, and your ring finger plays the 4th fret of the D string.

F # 7

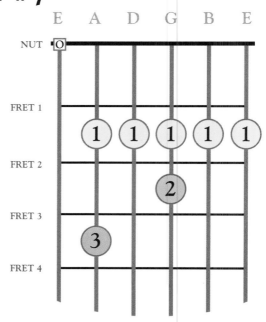

Let your index finger play across all 2nd frets of the E,B,G,D and A strings, and let your middle finger play the 3rd fret of the G string and your ring finger play the 4th fret of the A string.

F 6

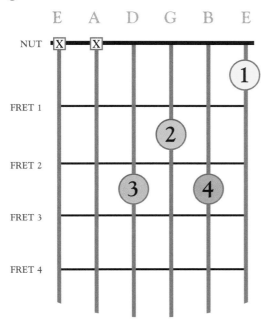

Let your index finger play 1st fret of the top E, your middle finger play the 2nd fret of the G string, your ring finger play the 3rd fret of the D string and your little finger play the 3rd fret of the B string.

F 9

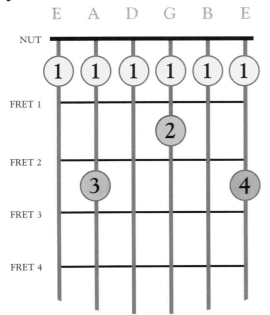

Use your index finger across the 1st fret of all six strings. Middle finger plays 2nd fret of the G string, ring finger plays 3rd fret of the A string and little finger plays the 3rd fret of the top E string.

USEFUL CHORDS: G

G

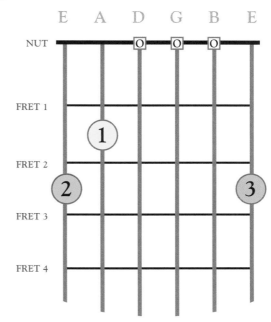

For the G chord let your index finger play the 2nd fret of the A string, your middle finger play the 3rd fret of the bottom E string and your ring finger play the 3rd fret of the top E string.

G 7

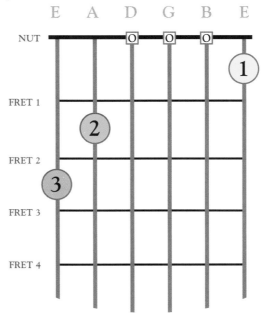

Your index finger should play the 1st fret of the E string, your middle finger should play the 2nd fret of the A string and your ring finger should play the 3rd fret of the bottom E string.

G Minor

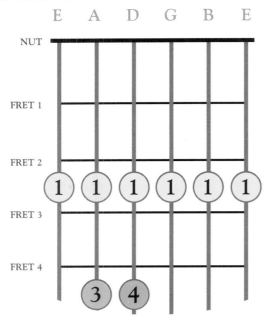

Use your index finger to play across all six strings at the 3rd fret. Let your ring finger play the 5th fret of the A string and your little finger play 5th fret of the D string.

G Flat Major 7

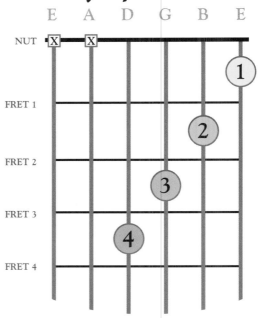

Use your index finger to play the 1st fret of the E string, your middle finger to play the 2nd fret of the B string, your ring finger to play the 3rd fret of the G string and your little finger to play the 4th fret of the D string.

G Major 7

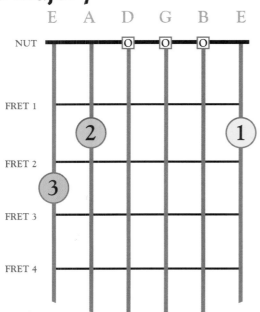

Use your index finger to play the 2nd fret of the top E string. Your middle finger plays the 2nd fret of the A string, and your ring finger should play the 3rd fret of the bottom E.

G Minor 7

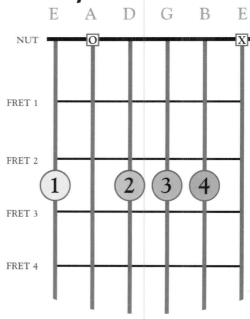

Use your index finger on the 3rd fret of the bottom E. Your middle finger plays the 3rd fret of the D string, ring finger plays 3rd fret of the G string and little finger plays the 3rd fret of the B string.

INDEX

MUSIC CREDITS

All Along The Watchtower
Words and Music by Bob Dylan. © 1968 Dwarf Music, USA. B Feldman and Co Ltd, London WC2H 0QY. Reproduced by permission of International Music Publications Ltd. All Rights Reserved.

All Day And All Of The Night
Written and composed by Ray Davies. © 1964 by Edward Kassner Music Co. Ltd. Copyright © 1964 Jayboy Music Corp. Copyright Renewed. All Rights Administered by Sony/ATV Music Publishing, 8 Music Square West, Nashville, TN 37203. International Copyright Secured. All Rights Reserved.

Black Night
Words and Music by Jon Lord, Ritchie Blackmore, Ian Gillan, Roger Glover and Ian Paice. © 1970 B Feldman and Co Ltd trading as Hec Music, London WC2H 0QY. Reproduced by permission of International Music Publications Ltd. All Rights for the United States and Canada Controlled and Administered by Glenwood Music Corp. For Australia and New Zealand: EMI Music Publishing Australia (ABN 83 000 040 951) PO Box 481, Spit Junction, NSW 2088, Australia. International copyright secured. All Rights Reserved. Used by Permission.

Bohemian Rhapsody
Words and Music by Freddie Mercury. © 1975 (Renewed 2003) B Feldman and Co Ltd trading as Trident Music Ltd, London WC2H 0QY. All Rights Controlled and Administered by Glenwood Music Corp. Reproduced by permission of International Music Publications Ltd. All Rights Reserved.

Brown Sugar
Written by Mick Jagger, Keith Richards. Published by ABKCO Music, Inc.

Cross Road Blues (Crossroads)
Words and Music by Robert Johnson. Copyright © (1978), 1990, 1991 Lehsem II, LLC and Claud L. Johnson. Administered by Music and Media International, Inc. International Copyright Secured. All Rights Reserved.

Dark Star
Words and Music by Jerry Garcia and Robert Hunter. © 1968 Ice Nine Publishing Co Inc, USA. Warner/Chappell North America Ltd, London W6 8BS. Reproduced by permission of International Music Publications Ltd. All Rights Reserved.

Get It On
Words and music by Marc Bolan. © 1971 Westminster Music Limited of Suite 1.07, Plaza 535 Kings Road, London SW10 0SZ. International Copyright Secured. All Rights Reserved. Used by Permission.

Heartbreak Hotel
Words and Music by Mae Boren Axton, Tommy Durden and Elvis Presley. Copyright © 1956 Sony/ATV Songs LLC. Copyright Renewed. All Rights Administered by Sony/ATV Music Publishing, 8 Music Square West, Nashville, TN 37203. International Copyright Secured. All Rights Reserved.

Heartbreaker
Words and Music by Jimmy Page, Robert Plant, John Paul Jones and John Bonham. © 1969 (renewed) Flames Of Albion Music Inc, USA. Warner/Chappell Music Ltd, London W6 8BS. Reproduced by permission of International Music Publications Ltd. All Rights Reserved.

Hey Joe
Words and Music by Billy Roberts. © 1962 Third Story Music Inc, USA. Carlin Music Corp, London NW1 8BD for PRS Territories only. Reproduced by permission of International Music Publications Ltd. All Rights Reserved.

I Ain't Superstitious
Words and Music by Willie Dixon. © Copyright 1963 Arc Music Corporation, USA. Tristan Music Limited. Used by permission of Music Sales Limited. All Rights Reserved. International Copyright Secured.

(I Can't Get No) Satisfaction
Written by Mick Jagger, Keith Richards. Published by ABKCO Music, Inc.

I've Found A New Baby
Words by Spencer Williams. Music by Jack Palmer. © 1926 Clarence Williams Music Publishing Co Inc and Pickwick Music Corp, USA (50%) B. Feldman and Co Ltd, London WC2H 0QY (50%). Redwood Music Ltd, London NW1 8BD for the Commonwealth of Nations, Germany, Austria, Switzerland, South Africa and Spain. Reproduced by permission of International Music Publications Ltd. All Rights Reserved.

Iron Man
Words and Music by Terence Butler, John Osbourne, Tony Iommi and William Ward. © 1969 Westminster Music Limited of Suite 2.07, Plaza 535 Kings Road, London SW10 0SZ.

Jessica
Words and Music by Forrest Richard Betts. © 1973 (renewed) Unichappell Music Inc and Forrest Richard Betts Music, USA. Warner/Chappell North America Ltd, London W6 8BS. Reproduced by permission of International Music Publications Ltd. All Rights Reserved.

Jumpin' Jack Flash
Written by Mick Jagger, Keith Richards. Published by ABKCO Music, Inc.

Kashmir
Words and Music by Jimmy Page, Robert Plant and John Bonham. © 1975 Flames Of Albion Music Inc, USA. Warner/Chappell Music Ltd, London W6 8BS. Reproduced by permission of International Music Publications Ltd. All Rights Reserved.

Layla
Words and Music by Eric Clapton and Jim Gordon. © Copyright 1970, 1998 and 2005 Eric Clapton and Throat Music Ltd. Used by permission of Music Sales Limited and International Music Publications Ltd. International Copyright Secured.

Le Freak
Words and Music by Bernard Edwards and Nile Rodgers. © Copyright 1979 Bernard's Other Music/Sony/ATV Songs LLC, USA. Warner/Chappell Music Limited (50%)/Sony/ATV Music Publishing (UK) Limited (50%). All Rights on behalf of Sony/ATV Songs LLC Administered by Sony/ATV Music Publishing, 8 Music Square West, Nashville, TN 37203. Used by permission of Music Sales Limited and International Music Publications Ltd. All Rights Reserved. International Copyright Secured.

Live And Let Die
Words and Music by Paul McCartney and Linda McCartney. © Copyright 1973 MPL Communications Limited (75%)/EMI United Partnership Limited, worldwide print rights controlled by Alfred Publishing/IMP Limited (25%). Used by permission of Music Sales Limited and International Music Publications Ltd. All Rights Reserved. International Copyright Secured.

Me And The Devil Blues
Words and Music by Robert Johnson. Copyright © (1978), 1990, 1991 Lehsem II, LLC and Claud L. Johnson. Administered by Music and Media International, Inc. International Copyright Secured All Rights Reserved.

Money
Words and Music by George Roger Waters. © 1973 Roger Waters Music Overseas Ltd. Warner/Chappell Artemis Music Ltd, London W6 8BS Reproduced by permission of International Music Publications Ltd. All Rights Reserved.

Mr Bojangles
Words and Music by Jerry Jeff Walker. © 1968 (renewed) Cotillion Music Inc and Mijac Music Inc, USA. Warner/Chappell North America Ltd, London W6 8BS. Reproduced by permission of International Music Publications Ltd. All Rights Reserved.

Mystery Train
Words and Music by Sam C Phillips and Herman Parker Jr. © 1955 (renewed) Hi-Lo Music and Mijac Music, USA. Carlin Music Corp, London NW1 8BD for the Commonwealth of Nations (excluding Canada/Australasia) Eire and Israel. Warner/Chappell North America Ltd, London W6 8BS for the Rest Of The World. Reproduced by permission of International Music Publications Ltd. All Rights Reserved.

Nuages
Music by Django Reinhardt and Jacques Larue. © 1980 Peter Maurice Music Ltd. All Rights for the U.S. and Canada Controlled and Administered by Colgems-EMI Music Inc. All Rights Reserved. International Copyright Secured. Used by Permission.

Paranoid
Words and Music by Terence Butler, John Osbourne, Tony Iommi and William Ward. © 1969 Westminster Music Limited of Suite 1.07, Plaza 535 Kings Road, London SW10 0SZ.

Phase Dance
Music by Pat Metheny and Lyle Mays. © Copyright 1978 Pat Meth Music Corporation and Lyle Mays Music, USA. BMG Music Publishing Limited. Used by permission of Music Sales Limited. All Rights Reserved. International Copyright Secured.

Pinball Wizard
Words and Music by Pete Townshend. Copyright © 1969 by Towser Tunes, Inc., ABKCO Music and Fabulous Music Ltd. Copyright Renewed. All Rights for Towser Tunes, Inc. administered by BMG Music Publishing International. All Rights for BMG Music Publishing International in the U.S. Administered by Careers-BMG Music Publishing, a division of BMG Music Publishing NA, Inc. International Copyright Secured. All Rights Reserved.

Pride And Joy
Written by Stevie Ray Vaughan. © 1985 Ray Vaughan Music (ASCAP)/Administered by Bug Music. All Rights Reserved. Used by Permission

Purple Rain
Words and Music by Prince. © Copyright 1984 Controversy Music, USA. All Rights Controlled and Administered by Universal Music Corp. Universal/MCA Music Limited. Used by permission of Music Sales Limited. All Rights Reserved. International Copyright Secured.

Rebel Rebel
Words and Music by David Bowie. © Copyright 1974 Jones Music America/RZO Music Limited (37.5%)/ Moth Music, Bewlay Brothers Music and EMI Music Publishing Ltd (37.5%)/Chrysalis Music Limited (25%). Used by permission of Music Sales Limited and International Music Publications Ltd. © 1974 Mainman Saag Ltd for Australia and New Zealand: EMI Music Publishing Australia Pty Limited (ABN 83 000 040 951) PO Box 481, Spit Junction, NSW 2088, Australia. All Rights for EMI Music Publishing Ltd controlled and administered by Colgems-EMI Music Inc. All Rights for Jones Music America administered by Arzo Publishing. All Rights for Moth Music administered by Chrysalis Songs. International copyright secured. All rights reserved. Used by Permission.

Ride A White Swan
Words and Music by Marc Bolan. © 1970 Westminster Music Limited of Suite 1.07, Plaza 535 Kings Road, London SW10 0SZ. International Copyright Secured. All Rights Reserved. Used by Permission.

River Man
Written by Nick Drake. © 1969 Warlock Music Ltd.

Scuttle Buttin'
Written by Stevie Ray Vaughan. © 1984 Ray Vaughan Music (ASCAP)/Administered by Bug Music. All Rights Reserved. Used by Permission.

Seven Nation Army
Words and Music by Jack White. © 2002 Peppermint Stripe Music (BMI), USA. EMI Music Publishing Ltd, London WC2H 0QY. Reproduced by permission of International Music Publications Ltd All Rights Reserved. Used by Permission.

She's Not There
Words and Music by Rod Argent. © 1964 Marquis Music Co Ltd, 1 Wyndham Yard, London W1H 2QF. Used by Permission.

Since You've Been Gone
Words and Music by Russ Ballard (Complete Music Ltd). © 1978 Complete Music Ltd. Printed by kind permission of Complete Music Ltd.

Smells Like Teen Spirit
Words and Music by Kurt Cobain, Krist Novoselic and Dave Grohl. © 1991 EMI Virgin Songs, Inc., The End of Music, M.J. Twelve Music and Murky Slough Music. All Rights Controlled and Administered by EMI Virgin Songs, Inc. All Rights Reserved. International Copyright Secured. Used by Permission.

Smoke On The Water
Words and Music by Jon Lord, Ritchie Blackmore, Ian Gillan, Roger Glover and Ian Paice. © 1972 B Feldman and Co Ltd trading as Hec Music, London WC2H 0QY. All Rights for the United States and Canada Controlled and Administered by Glenwood Music Corp. For Australia and New Zealand: EMI Music Publishing Australia Pty Limited (ABN 83 000 040 951) PO Box 481, Spit Junction, NSW 2088, Australia. International Copyright Secured. All Rights Reserved. Used by Permission.

Smooth
Words and Music by Itaal Shur and Robert Thomas. © 1999 Itaal Shur Music and Bidnis Inc, USA (60%) Warner/Chappell Music Ltd, London W6 8BS (40%) EMI Music Publishing Ltd, London WC2H 0QY. © 1999 EMI Blackwood Music, Inc., Bidnis, Inc. and Itaal Shur Music. All Rights for Bidnis, Inc. controlled and administered by EMI Blackwood Music, Inc. Reproduced by permission of International Music Publications Ltd. All Rights Reserved. International Copyright Secured. Used by Permission.

St Stephen
Words and Music by Robert Hunter, Jerry Garcia and Phil Lesh. © 1968 Ice Nine Publishing Co Inc, USA. Warner/Chappell North America Ltd, London W6 8BS. Reproduced by permission of International Music Publications Ltd. All Rights Reserved.

Stairway To Heaven
Words and Music by Jimmy Page and Robert Plant. © 1972 Superhype Music Inc, USA. Warner/Chappell Music Ltd, London W6 8BS. Reproduced by permission of International Music Publications Ltd. All Rights Reserved.

Start Me Up
Words and Music by Mick Jagger and Keith Richards. © 1978 Promopub BV, Netherlands. EMI Music Publishing Ltd, London WC2H 0QY. Reproduced by permission of International Music Publications Ltd. All Rights Reserved.

Stormy Monday Blues
Words and Music by Aaron 'T-Bone' Walker. Copyright © 1947; Renewed 1975 Gregmark Music, Inc. (BMI). Worldwide Rights excluding the British Reversionary Territories but including Canada for Gregmark Music, Inc. Administered by Cherry River Music Co. International Copyright Secured. All Rights Reserved.

Sunshine Of Your Love
Words and Music by Jack Bruce, Pete Brown and Eric Clapton. © Copyright 1967 and 1996 Eric Clapton (33.33%)/Warner/Chappell Music Limited (66.67%). Copyright © 1968, 1973 by Dratleaf Ltd. Copyright Renewed. All Rights Administered by Unichappell Music Inc. Used by permission of Music Sales Limited and International Music Publications Ltd. All Rights Reserved.

Sweet Baby James
Words and Music by James Taylor. © 1970 (Renewed 1998) EMI Blackwood Music Inc. and Country Road Music Inc. All Rights Controlled and Administered by EMI Blackwood Music Inc. All Rights Reserved. International Copyright Secured. Used by Permission

Sweet Little Angel
Words and Music by B.B. King and Jules Bihari. Copyright © 1956 Careers-BMG Music Publishing, a division of BMG Music Publishing NA, Inc. Copyright Renewed. International Copyright Secured. All Rights Reserved.

Sweet Sixteen
Words and Music by B.B. King and Joe Bihari. Copyright © 1967 Careers-BMG Music Publishing, a division of BMG Music Publishing NA, Inc. Copyright Renewed. International Copyright Secured. All Rights Reserved.

Three O'Clock Blues
Words and Music by B.B. King and Jules Bihari. Copyright © 1952 Careers-BMG Music Publishing, a division of BMG Music Publishing NA, Inc. Copyright Renewed. International Copyright Secured. All Rights Reserved.

Tie Your Mother Down
Words and Music by Brian May. © 1976 Queen Music Ltd, London WC2H 0QY./ All Rights for the U.S. and Canada controlled and administered by Beechwood Music Corp. All Rights for the World excluding the U.S. and Canada controlled and administered by EMI Music Publishing Ltd. Reproduced by permission of International Music Publications Ltd. All Rights Reserved.

Time
Words and Music by George Roger Waters, David Gilmour, Nicholas Mason and Richard Wright. © 1973 Roger Waters Music Overseas Ltd and Pink Floyd Music Publishers Ltd (25%) Warner/Chappell Artemis Music Ltd, London W6 8BS. Reproduced by permission of International Music Publications Ltd. All Rights Reserved.

Tired Of Waiting For You
Written and composed by Ray Davies. © 1964 by Edward Kassner Music Co. Ltd. Copyright Renewed. All Rights Administered by Sony/ATV Music Publishing, 8 Music Square West, Nashville, TN 37203. International Copyright Secured. All Rights Reserved.

Travels
Words and Music by Pat Metheny and Lyle Mays. © Copyright BMG Music Publishing Limited. Used by permission of Music Sales Limited. All Rights Reserved. International Copyright Secured.

We Will Rock You
Words and Music by Brian May. © 1977 Queen Music Ltd, London WC2H 0QY. All Rights for the U.S. and Canada controlled and administered by Beechwood Music Corp. All Rights for the World excluding the U.S. and Canada controlled and administered by EMI Music Publishing Ltd. Reproduced by permission of International Music Publications Ltd. All Rights Reserved.

Where Were You?
Words and Music by Jeff Beck, Terry Bozzio and Tony Hymas. © 1989 BHB Music Ltd, USA. Warner/Chappell North America Ltd, London W6 8BS. Reproduced by permission of International Music Publications Ltd. All Rights Reserved.

Who Do You Love
Words and Music by Ellas McDaniel. © Copyright 1956 (renewed), 1991 Arc Music Corporation (BMI). Tristan Music Limited. Used by permission of Music Sales Limited. All Rights Reserved. International Copyright Secured.

Whole Lotta Love
Words and Music by Jimmy Page, Robert Plant, John Bonham, John Paul Jones and Willie Dixon. © 1970 Flames Of Albion Music Inc, USA. Warner/Chappell Music Ltd, London W6 8BS. Reproduced by permission of International Music Publications Ltd. All Rights Reserved.

Wildwood Flower
Words and Music by A.P. Carter. © Copyright 1935 Peer International Corporation, USA. Peermusic (UK) Limited. Copyright Renewed. Used by permission of Music Sales Limited. All Rights Reserved. International Copyright Secured.

Wish You Were Here
Words and Music by George Roger Waters and David Gilmour. © 1975 Roger Waters Music Overseas Ltd and Pink Floyd Music Publishers Ltd (50%) Warner/Chappell Artemis Music Ltd, London W6 8BS. Reproduced by permission of International Music Publications Ltd. All Rights Reserved.

The Yellow Princess
Words and Music by John Fahey. © 1966 Terraplin Music. Carlin Music Corp, London, NW1 8BD for the Commonwealth of Nations (excluding Canada/Australasia) and Eire.

You Really Got Me
Written and composed by Ray Davies. © 1964 by Edward Kassner Music Co. Ltd. Copyright © 1964 Jayboy Music Corp. Copyright Renewed. All Rights Administered by Sony/ATV Music Publishing, 8 Music Square West, Nashville, TN 37203. International Copyright Secured. All Rights Reserved.

You've Got A Friend
Words and Music by Carole King. © 1971 (Renewed 1999) Colgems-EMI Music Inc. All Rights Reserved. International Copyright Secured. Used by Permission.

Ziggy Stardust
Words and Music by David Bowie. © Copyright 1972 Tintoretto Music/RZO Music Ltd (37.5%)/ Moth Music, Bewlay Brothers Music Ltd (37.5%)/Chrysalis Music Ltd, (25%). Used by permission of Music Sales Limited and International Music Publications Ltd. International Copyright Secured. © 1972 Mainman Saag Ltd for Australia and New Zealand: EMI Music Publishing Australia Pty Limited (ABN 83 000 040 951) PO Box 481, Spit Junction, NSW 2088, Australia. All Rights for EMI Music Publishing Ltd. Controlled and administered by Screen Gems-EMI Music Inc. All Rights for Tintoretto Music administered by RZO Music. All Rights for Moth Music administered by Chrysalis Songs. International Copyright Secured. All Rights Reserved. Used by Permission.

Every effort has been made to contact the copyright holders for all music used in this book. If you believe that you are the copyright holder and have not been approached, please contact Amber Books Ltd.

PHOTOGRAPHY CREDITS

All studio photography © Amber Books Ltd

Dorling Kindersley: 46 (top – Dave King)

Fender Europe: 7 (left)

Getty Images: 13 (Frank Micelotta), 124 (Keystone Features / Hulton Archive), 132 (Frank Micelotta), 148 (Sebastian Artz), 164 (Sebastian Artz), 180 (Miguel Rojo / AFP), 191 (Frank Driggs), 199 (Frank Driggs), 229 (Eric Schaal / Time & Life Pictures)

Guitar Traders: 70 (courtesy Mr. Naoki Washida)

Keith Morris: 233, 239, 240

Redferns: 8 (David Redfern), 9 (Michael Ochs), 10 (Ian Dickson), 11 (David Redfern), 12 (Richard Ecclestone), 15–16 (Michael Ochs), 19 (Don Paulsen), 20 (Bernd Muller), 22 (David Redfern), 24 (Bob King), 26 (Paul Bergen), 32 (Ebet Roberts), 34 (David Redfern), 37 (David Redfern), 38 (K & K Ulf Kruger), 40 (Robert Knight), 43 (Richard E. Aaron), 44 (Ian Dickson), 46 (bottom – Grant Davis), 48 (Richard E. Aaron), 53 (GEMS), 54 (Michael Ochs), 57 (Mick Hutson), 58 (David Redfern), 61 (Ebet Roberts), 62 (Michael Ochs), 67 (David Redfern), 68 (Mick Hutson), 73 (Ron Howard), 79 (Fotex Agentur), 80 (Robert Knight), 82 (Jim McCary), 85 (David Redfern), 86 (Paul Reed Smith), 88 (bottom – David Redfern), 91 (Ebet Roberts), 92 (Fin Costello), 94 (Andrew Lepley), 99 (Richard E. Aaron), 100 (Fin Costello), 102 (Ebet Roberts), 105 (Harry Goodwin), 106 (Ian Dickson), 108 (Colin Fuller), 111 (Alain Dister), 114 (Richard Ecclestone), 118 (David Redfern), 119 (Phil Dent), 120 (Geoff Dann), 122 (Bob King), 127–128 (Ebet Roberts), 131 (Richard E. Aaron), 135–136 (Mick Hutson), 139 (Peter Pakvis), 140 (Ebet Roberts), 143 (Tabatha Fireman), 144 (Paul Reed Smith), 146 (Michael Ochs), 147 (Deltahaze Corporation), 149–150 (David Redfern), 151 (Chuck Stewart), 153–154 (Deltahaze Corporation), 156 (Leon Morris), 159 (Jan Persson), 160 (Michael Ochs), 163 (Mick Hutson), 166 (Michael Ochs), 168 (David Redfern), 171–173 (David Redfern), 175 (Ebet Roberts), 176 (Richard E. Aaron), 178 (Don Paulsen), 183 (Ebet Roberts), 184 (Robert Knight), 186 (David Redfern), 188 (Michael Ochs), 192 (Bob Willoughby), 195 (Michael Ochs), 196 (Paul Reed Smith), 200 (William Gottlieb), 203 (Mick Hutson), 204 (Bob Willoughby), 206 (Robert Knight), 208–211 (Michael Ochs), 212 (Geoff Dann), 215 (Michael Ochs), 216 (Geoff Dann), 219 (Michael Ochs), 220 (Paul Reed Smith), 223–224 (Michael Ochs), 226 (Michael Ochs), 230 (Michael Ochs), 235 (Ebet Roberts), 236 (Michael Ochs)

Rex Features: 29 (Andre Csillag), 30 (Alan Messer), 64 (Andre Csillag), 74 (Alan Messer), 76 (London Weekend Television), 96 (Andre Csillag)